Plays of People at Work

Published by Smith and Kraus, Inc.
PO Box 127, Lyme, NH 03768

Copyright ©1998 by L.E. McCullough

CAUTION: Professionals and amateurs are hereby warned that the plays represented in this book are subject to a royalty. They are fully protected under the copyright laws of the United States of America, and of all countries covered by the International Copyright Union (including the Dominion of Canada and the rest of the British Commonwealth), and of all countries covered by the Pan-American Copyright Convention and the Universal Copyright Convention, and of all countries with which the United States has reciprocal copyright relations. All rights, including professional, amateur, motion picture, recitation, lecturing, radio broadcasting, television, video or sound taping, all other forms of mechanical or electronic reproductions such as CD-ROM and CD-I, information storage and retrieval systems and photocopying, and the rights of translation into foreign languages, are strictly reserved. Please contact Smith and Kraus for any questions concerning rights.

Performance Rights: These plays may be performed in classrooms and schools without charge. Any other performances require written permission and the payment of a fee. For permission contact Smith and Kraus, Inc. PO Box 127, Lyme, NH 03768. Tel. (603) 643-6431.

Manufactured in the United States of America
First Edition: December 1998
10 9 8 7 6 5 4 3 2 1

Cover and text design by Julia Hill Gignoux/Freedom Hill Design
Front cover photos, from top: Michael Vaughn, Communications and Publications of Indiana University-Purdue University at Indianapolis, Shawn Spence, Communications and Publications of Indiana University-Purdue University at Indianapolis, and L.E. McCullough.
Back cover photos, from top: Shawn Spence, Michael Vaughn, and Purdue School of Engineering and Technology at IUPUI.

The Library of Congress Cataloging-In-Publication Data
McCullough, L.E.
Plays of People at Work: grades K–3 / L.E. McCullough.
p. cm. — (Young actors series)

Summary: A collection of twelve plays in which Janice, Steve, Paula, and Burton investigate a variety of occupations, including newspaper reproter, robotics engineer, and crime lab technician.

ISBN 1-57525-140-X
1. Labor—Juvenile drama. 2. Children's plays, American.
[1. Occupations—Drama. 2. Plays.] I. Title. II. Series: Young actors series.

PS3563.C35297P586   1998
812'.54—dc21   98-44104
                      CIP
                      AC

Plays of **People** at **Work**

Grades K–3

L.E. McCullough

YOUNG ACTORS SERIES

SK
A Smith and Kraus book

Dedication

This book is dedicated to my parents, who let my life's work emerge bright and clear through the murky haze of adolescence; to Nicholas Berchem, who painted masterworks to the beat of a banging broom; and to every working person throughout history who has struggled to gain dignity and fair value for their labor.

Contents

Monster in the Basement *(Animal Rescue Agent)*...... 1

The Big Scoop *(Newspaper Reporter)* 10

Roll 'em Up, Roll 'em Up! *(Pastry Chef)* 23

Call of the Wild *(Park Ranger)*................... 34

Opening Night at the Opera, er, Opry *(Piano Tuner)* 45

It's an Emergency! *(Emergency Medical Technician)*.... 56

Robots Are Everywhere *(Robotics Engineer)*........ 66

Heave Away, Haul Away! *(Tugboat Captain)* 77

The Case of the Purple Pen *(Crime Lab Technician)* .. 99

See You in Court! *(Legal Aid Lawyer)* 112

Yankee Doodle Had a Brick *(Brick Mason)*......... 124

Lights, Camera, Traction! *(Television Director)* 136

Reach for the Stars *(Epilogue)* 149

Acknowledgments

Some significant work mentors over the years: my high school band teachers Jim Zarnowiecki and William Grimes; Bertha and Orpha at G.C. Murphy's; Elmer Spivey, foreman at Bon Ami; James Egan, the manager at Flaming Hearth; Bill Baugh of Battle Ground Historical Society; Denny of Caz' Cafe; Kathleen George of City Theatre; the Gormley Bros. of Frankie Gustine's; Brian Cunningham of Dooley O'Toole's; Michael of Colorado Street Cafe; Miles Krassen of Oberlin University; bandleaders Serge Lainé, Noel Rice, Larry Edelman, and Ernie Hawkins; W.K. McNeil, Jeffrey Huntsman, and Carlos Boilés of Indiana University; Dan Weinberg and Chico Fernandez of WFBM-TV; Rene Studebaker of the *Austin American-Statesman;* Mary Lavin of the School of Irish Studies; Dave Samuelson of Puritan Records; Tom Evans of Hanover College; David Hochoy of Dance Kaleidoscope; pipemaker Patrick Hennelly; Carol Robertson at University of Maryland; Joe and Anne Englander; Kay Keesee; Jim Williams; Gloria Moore; Jim Hudson; Ann Stack of Arts Indiana; Darrell Bailey and Jim Brown of IUPUI; Claude McNeal of American Cabaret Theatre.

Foreword

All of a sudden and out of nowhere a child shows who she is, what he must do.
— James Hillman
The Soul's Code

The hardest work some people do is describing the work they do.
— E.C. McKenzie, humorist

The plays in this book respond to children's number one query about their future lives as working adults: "What will I do when I grow up?"

Plays of People at Work follows a quartet of bright, inquisitive grade-schoolers as they visit friends and family at real-life work sites to learn about contemporary, gender-neutral occupations. These plays are a perfect complement to any "career day" program and can serve as a starting point for discussion about children's occupational aptitudes and the skills and training needed to be a productive member of the modern global workplace.

In terms of physical description, the main characters have been left vague — purposely. Janice, Steve, Paula, and Burton can be *any* ethnicity, *any* religion, *any* social class, *any* size or shape and can be played by *any* child, even those with physical or mental disabilities. They are, pure and simple, American children at the turn of the twenty-first century, and this breadth of characterization should give play presenters the freedom to utilize the talents of any child in the company or classroom.

Plays of People at Work has been designed to combine with studies in other disciplines: history, science, language, dance, music, social studies, etc. *Call of the Wild* and *Monster in the Basement* can supplement lesson plans in ecology and wildlife. *Robots Are Everywhere* can generate a pre- or post-play discussion about the evolution of technology and the role it plays in our lives. Feel free to decorate the set with architecture, plants, and art objects specific to that job site. If you are a music teacher and want to add songs and music to any of the plays, go ahead and make it a class project by organizing a chorus or having students select appropriate recordings of occupational work songs to play before and after the performance.

If you want to introduce more detailed information into your presentation of the plays, consult *Career Information Center,* a thirteen-volume series listing hundreds of contemporary occupations published by MacMillan and found in libraries at call number 331.702 (internet address: http://www.umsl.edu/services/govdocs/ooh9899/1.htm). Your local library will certainly have other books and videos on individual jobs that can enhance your group's playmaking.

Besides those children enrolled in the onstage cast, others can be included in the production as lighting and sound technicians, prop masters, script coaches, and stage managers. *Plays of People at Work* is an excellent vehicle for getting other members of the school and community involved in your project. There are undoubtedly knowledgeable workers in these occupations in your area who can add interesting stories about their jobs. Try utilizing the talents of local school or youth orchestra members to play incidental music...get the school art club to paint scrims and backdrops...see if a senior citizens' group might volunteer time to sew costumes...inquire whether any local businesses might bring posters, brochures, or samples of their products.

Most of all, have lots of fun. Realizing that many performing groups may have limited technical and space resources, I have kept sets, costumes, and props minimal. However, if you do have the ability to fashion a facsimile television news studio for *Lights, Camera, Traction!* or build an entire police crime lab for *The Case of the Purple Pen* — go for it! Adding more music and dance and visual arts and crafts into the production involves more children and makes your play a genuinely multimedia event.

Similarly, I have supplied only basic stage and lighting directions. Blocking is really the province of the director; once you get the play up and moving, feel free to suit cast and action to your available population and experience level of actors. When figuring out how to stage these plays, I suggest you follow the venerable UYI Method — Use Your Imagination. If the play calls for a boat, bring in a wood frame, an old bathtub, or have children draw a boat and hang it as a scrim behind where the actors perform. Keep in mind the spirit of the old Andy Hardy musicals: "C'mon, everybody! Let's make a show!"

Age and gender. Obviously, your purpose in putting on the play is to entertain as well as educate; even though one typically thinks of castle guards and king's soldiers as being male, there is no reason these roles can't be played in *your* production by females; likewise for witches, ogres, and trolls. After all, the essence of the theatrical experience is to suspend us in time and ask us to believe that anything may be possible. Once again, UYI! Adult characters can certainly be played by children costumed or made up to fit the part as closely as possible, or they can actually be played by adults. While *Plays of People at Work* are intended to be performed chiefly by children, moderate adult involvement will add validation and let children know this isn't just a time-killing "kid project." If you want to get very highly choreographed or musically intensive, you will probably find a strategically placed onstage adult or two very helpful in keeping things moving smoothly. Still, *never* underestimate the capacity for even the youngest children to amaze you with their skill and ingenuity in making a show blossom.

Plays of People at Work is a great way to enliven one of the richest life-shaping experiences in which a child can participate. And for adults, these plays offer a chance to recapture the joy and excitement we all felt the first time we discovered our true calling and heard our inner soul exclaim, "Eureka! This is for me!"

L.E. McCullough, Ph.D.
Humanities Theatre Group
Indiana University-Purdue
University at Indianapolis
Indianapolis, Indiana

Plays of **People at Work**

Monster in the Basement
(Animal Rescue Agent)

Many people who work as animal rescue agents (a field sometimes humorously referred to as "critter control") come to the job simply because they enjoy working with animals. Other animal rescue agents are engaged in a more serious mission — to preserve the natural balance between animals and people in our shared habitat. As towns and cities have moved further into what were formerly wilderness areas, "wild" animals such as raccoons, woodchucks, beavers, bats, skunks, moles, deer, and even alligators and coyotes have become commonplace in densely populated urban and suburban neighborhoods. When these animals seek food and shelter in people's homes, they can be a nuisance and also suffer harm themselves. Animal rescue agents gently capture the animals and then either treat them for injuries or, if unharmed, release them back into a more wild area. Most animal rescue agents are self-employed, though some work with local veterinarians and animal shelters. Animal rescue agents must know a great deal about the feeding and nesting habits of birds and animals, and some people working in the field have taken college courses in zoology, biology, and animal husbandry.

For information about animal rescue agents and urban wildlife, call your local Humane Society or consult these web sites:

http://www.applink.net/~shurtlef/arl/animals/anmlctrl.html (Animal Rescue League)
http://www.hsus.org/ (Humane Society of the United States)
http://www.cc.ndsu.nodak.edu/instruct/devold/twrid/html/index.htm (Wildlife Rehabilitation Information Directory)

RUNNING TIME: 15 minutes

CAST: 10 actors, minimum 4 boys (•), 5 girls (+)

- + Paula
- • Burton
- + Janice
- • Steve
- + Ms. Vera, Teacher
- • Art Dawson, Animal Rescue Agent
- + Sandi Barr, Art's Assistant
- • Mr. Cogan
- + Mrs. Cogan
- Rocky Raccoon (actor behind scrim)

STAGE SET: scrim or curtain at mid center; small table at down left with toolbox adjacent

PROPS: toolbox, wire pet cage, spoon, needle-nose pliers, food bowl, flashlight, a three-foot-long pole, two pairs of heavy work gloves, toy raccoon (to simulate live raccoon)

MUSIC: "Raccoon, Raccoon, Come into My Room"

COSTUMES: Paula, Burton, Janice, and Steve wear standard grade-school attire (Spring season); Burton wears a baseball cap and Janice has a bookbag on her back; Ms. Vera wears a standard female teacher's school outfit; Art Dawson and Sandi Barr wear jeans, dark T-shirts and work boots; Mr. Cogan dresses in plaid shirt, black slacks, and loafers; Mrs. Cogan wears floral print dress and sandals.

```
*** UPSTAGE ***
Right              Center                    Left
```

                    Mr.   Mrs.
                   Cogan Cogan [cage]
                   [scrim/curtain]
                                              Art Hanley
                                              [table] Sandi
            Burton   Steve   [toolbox]
    Paula   Janice   Ms. Vera

Stage Plan —*Monster in the Basement*

(actor positions at entrance)

Key: ▬▬▬ scrim or curtain   ☐ table
         ▨▨▨ cage   ▦▦▦ toolbox

(LIGHTS UP RIGHT on PAULA, BURTON, JANICE, and STEVE standing at down right, singing "Raccoon, Raccoon, Come into My Room.")

PAULA, BURTON, JANICE & STEVE: *(sing)*
    Raccoon, raccoon, come into my room
    I'll give you a slice of bacon;
    And when I bake, I'll give you a cake
    If I am not mistaken.

(MS. VERA enters from right.)

MS. VERA: Good morning, class!

PAULA, BURTON, JANICE, & STEVE: Good morning, Ms. Vera!

MS. VERA: Isn't this a beautiful day for a field trip? This morning we're going to meet an animal rescue agent. He'll take us along on a real rescue. *(looks toward down left)* There he is now! *(waves)* Hello, Mr. Dawson!

(LIGHTS UP CENTER AND LEFT on ART DAWSON and SANDI BARR standing at down left next to a table, on which there is a midsized wire pet cage. Art Dawson is using needle-nose pliers to adjust the cage door and Sandi, wearing heavy work gloves, is using a spoon to mix something in a food bowl. Ms. Vera leads the class to down left to greet them.)

ART DAWSON: Hi, there! My name is Art Dawson. This is my assistant, Sandi Barr.

SANDI BARR: Hi, there!

ART DAWSON: We are animal rescue agents. Our job is to find animals that have gotten lost and wandered into people's homes.

SANDI BARR: Or been caught in traps.

ART DAWSON: Then we take them back to their real homes in nature.

JANICE: *(raises hand)* What kind of animals do you rescue?

ART DAWSON: Almost every kind that crawls, flies or swims.

PAULA: *(raises hand)* Squirrels?

ART DAWSON: Quite a few in the fall.

STEVE: *(raises hand)* Birds?

SANDI BARR: They often fly down chimneys and become stuck.

BURTON: *(raises hand)* How about snakes?

ART DAWSON: I've got a thirty-foot African python in the back of my truck right now.

(*Kids shout all at once; Art Dawson and Sandi Barr laugh.*)

PAULA: Oooh!
BURTON: Wow!
JANICE: Gross!
STEVE: Cool!
SANDI BARR: He's just joking, kids. But yesterday we did rescue a very confused green snake from the inside of a mailbox.
ART DAWSON: And now we're here at the home of Mr. and Mrs. Cogan.

(*An elderly couple, MR. COGAN and MRS. COGAN, enter from behind scrim/curtain and stand at mid center; they approach Art Dawson, Mrs. Cogan very agitated and Mr. Cogan very calm.*)

MRS. COGAN: Oh, thank goodness, you're here! There's a monster in our basement!
MR. COGAN: Now, Evelyn, it's probably just —
MRS. COGAN: The most horrifying noise you can imagine! All night long for three whole days!
MR. COGAN: It *does* make quite a racket, scratching up a storm round midnight or so.
MRS. COGAN: At first I thought some awful burglar had broken in!
MR. COGAN: Doesn't smell like a burglar, though. Smells more like — (*sniffs twice*) — fresh coffee and fried bacon.

MRS. COGAN: I can't stand the thought of having whatever it is in my basement!

MR. COGAN: I'm not so sure it wants to be there, either. Sounds like it's looking for a way out but can't find one. It's a pretty high drop from the window ledge to the basement floor.

ART DAWSON: We'll take a peek. *(puts on heavy work gloves)* Sandi, hand me the light and pole, please.

(Sandi Barr takes a flashlight and pole from the toolbox and hands it to Art Dawson, who goes to the leftmost edge of the scrim, bends down, and cautiously looks behind the scrim, gingerly poking with the pole and exploring with the flashlight.)

MRS. COGAN: Oh, you'll need more than that! You'll need a shotgun! A harpoon! Maybe a bazooka!

SANDI BARR: Mrs. Cogan, we don't want to hurt whatever is in your basement.

MRS. COGAN: You don't? Why not?

SANDI BARR: Because it likely doesn't want to hurt you.

MR. COGAN: Really? I would, if I were it.

STEVE: *(raises hand)* But, Ms. Barr, what if it *is* a monster? I mean, some gnarly creature that could eat Mrs. Cogan's legs off with one quick bite?

MS. VERA: Steven!

SANDI BARR: That's a very important point. These days so many people build houses where animals are used to hunting for food. The animals' natural habitat has been taken away, so they end up trying to live and feed where people do.

(Art Dawson rises and returns to table, handing flashlight and pole to Sandi Barr.)

ART DAWSON: I think I've found your monster.

MRS. COGAN: Oh, thank goodness! Is it a mountain lion? Or a bear?

ART DAWSON: Nope. Any guesses, kids?

STEVE: *(raises hand)* If it only moves around at night, it's an animal that sleeps during the day.

PAULA: *(raises hand)* If you hear scratching, it probably has paws.

BURTON: *(raises hand)* If it smells like bacon and coffee, it's probably been in the garbage.

JANICE: *(raises hand)* If the floor is a long way to the window, it can't jump very high.

(Paula, Burton, Janice, and Steve look at each other, then shout:)

PAULA, BURTON, JANICE, & STEVE: It's a raccoon!

ART DAWSON: You got it!

MRS. COGAN: Oh, my goodness! *(swoons, is caught by Mr. Cogan and revived)*

MS. VERA: How will you get it to come out?

ART DAWSON: Offer it a nice raccoon treat — a bowl of fresh cat food.

(Art Dawson takes the cage to the edge of the scrim; Sandi Barr puts the bowl in the cage; Art Dawson puts the cage behind the scrim; they both slowly back away.)

ART DAWSON: Usually we'd have to wait until night for it to come out, but this may not take so long. It's probably very hungry.

MR. COGAN: Worked up quite an appetite, I'd say. Only thing to eat in our basement are a heap of *National Geographics*.

(The cage begins rattling as squealing and trilling noises are heard.)

ROCKY RACCOON: *(behind scrim)* R-r-r-r-r! R-r-r-r-r! Eeeealll! Eeeealll!

SANDI BARR: Here comes Rocky Raccoon!

(Art Dawson goes behind scrim, brings out the cage, and holds it aloft, showing a live raccoon.)

ART DAWSON: Here's your monster, ma'am!

(Mrs. Cogan recoils, Mr. Cogan chuckles, kids "ooh" and "aah.")

SANDI BARR: I suppose we should check to see if she had any babies. It appears Rocky is a girl.

MRS. COGAN: Babies! *(swoons, is caught by Mr. Cogan and revived)*

(Art Dawson sets cage on table; kids and Ms. Vera gather round to look at raccoon.)

PAULA: That is awesome!

BURTON: I've never seen a live raccoon before.

STEVE: Me, either. Only in cartoons.

JANICE: What will you do with her?

ART DAWSON: Go to the woods at the edge of town and let her loose. I'm sure she'll find that a lot more hospitable than a dank old basement.

MR. COGAN: Thanks for getting that critter. We'll sleep a lot easier now.

SANDI BARR: Glad we could help. And thank you for not panicking and hurting her. Some people think of wildlife as an enemy. But we have to respect nature, or it won't be part of our world very much longer.

MRS. COGAN: *(fanning herself)* With all this excitement, I may not be part of the world much longer.

MR. COGAN: Nonsense, Evelyn. You'll be fine just as long as raccoons can't fire bazookas.

(Everyone laughs. LIGHTS OUT.)

THE END

The Big Scoop*
(Newspaper Reporter)

Newspaper reporters are journalists — persons whose job is to collect news and keep the public informed about important events. Journalists may work for newspapers, magazines, and radio and television stations writing news stories or opinion columns that comment on the news. A reporter's primary task is to get as many facts as possible about a subject and then check to see that the facts are accurate before the story is written and printed or broadcast. A good reporter has many of the same qualities found in detective work: determination, attention to detail, and the ability to easily obtain information from people who may be shy or otherwise unwilling to talk to strangers. Above all, a good reporter must be accurate and fair when writing a story, taking care to present the facts without bias or innuendo. Most full-time newspaper reporters graduate from college with a degree in journalism and typically began writing articles for their middle school or high school publications. It's never too young to start writing: Many local newspapers use articles written by part-time reporters called "stringers" and "freelancers"... if the news is hot and the writing clear and correct, they'll run your story!

Your local university or community college likely has some journalism courses. For information about newspaper reporting, contact these organizations:

http://www.uiowa.edu/~quill-sc/index.html (Quill and Scroll, the International Honorary Society for High School Journalists)

http://www.ire.org/index.html (Investigative Reporters and Editors, 138 Neff Annex, the Missouri School of Journalism, Columbia, MO 65211-1200. 573/882-2042.)

* "Getting the scoop" is when a journalist reports an exciting news story before anyone else; it was a term first used in the 1890s by newspaper reporters who often went to great lengths to break a story before reporters at rival newspapers.

RUNNING TIME: 15 minutes

CAST: 10 actors, minimum 4 boys (•), 6 girls (+)

+ Paula
• Burton
+ Janice
• Steve
• Bobby, Teenage Bystander
+ Mrs. Brown (Paula's Stepmother), a Newspaper Reporter
• Mr. Tapinszki, Soda Shop Owner
+ Ms. Calescu, Magazine Stand Owner
+ Sheila Bretkoff, Teenage Bystander
+ Officer D. Rau, Policewoman

STAGE SET: scrim or curtain at front of stage; town street set behind scrim — at mid right a soda shop, at mid center a sign pole (without sign) with upended motor scooter at base, at mid left a magazine stand; this street tableaux can be painted on a second scrim with upraised or hung signs ("Soda Shop" or "Magazine Stand") or it can be represented simply with tables and chairs and a pole

PROPS: motor scooter, motorcycle helmet, crumpled magazines and newspapers, umbrella, pen, notebook, micro-cassette tape recorder, wooden sign that reads "Today's Special Flavor"

EFFECTS: Sound — lightning, thunder and wind noise offstage; Visual — lights flicker to simulate lightning; Wind Gusts — large fans in the wings blowing across stage

COSTUMES: Paula, Burton, Janice, and Steve wear standard grade-school attire (Spring season); Burton wears a baseball cap and Janice has a bookbag on her back; Mrs. Brown wears a standard woman's business suit and skirt with jacket and carries a midsized purse; Mr. Tapinszki wears an ice cream clerk's uniform: white shirt, white pants, white apron, white shoes; Ms. Calescu wears a basic sales clerk's outfit, a dress or blouse and slacks; Sheila Bretkoff and Bobby wear contemporary teen clothes; Officer D. Rau wears police uniform and dark sunglasses

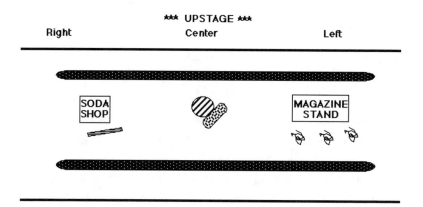

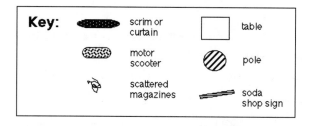

Stage Plan — *The Big Scoop*

12 PLAYS OF PEOPLE AT WORK

(FRONT SCRIM OR CURTAIN IS DOWN; LIGHTS UP FULL as PAULA, STEVE, BURTON, and JANICE enter stage from left with Paula leading; they pause at down center.)

STEVE: Hey, Paula! What time is your stepmom coming from the newspaper?
PAULA: She said to be in front of the soda shop at three-thirty.
BURTON: It sure is nice of her to take us out for ice cream.
JANICE: We're supposed to be watching her *work*, Burton — she didn't say anything about ice cream.
BURTON: Then why would she meet us in front of the soda shop, Janice?
STEVE: Then why did the gum cross the road, Burton?
JANICE: Excuse me, Steve?
BURTON: Because it was stuck to the chicken's foot!

(Burton, Paula, and Steve laugh.)

STEVE: Then why did the elephant cross the road?
PAULA: Because he was tied to the chicken!

(Burton, Paula, and Steve laugh.)

JANICE: Okay, smarty-pants: Why did the rooster cross the road?

(Burton, Paula, and Steve do not answer.)

JANICE: Because the chicken was on vacation! *(giggles)*
PAULA: *(deadpan)* Ha.
STEVE: *(deadpan)* Ha.
BURTON: *(deadpan)* Ha.

(SOUND EFFECT: Distant thunder rumbles.)

JANICE: Wow, it looks like a storm is coming. *(points skyward, above left)* Look at those big dark clouds!
STEVE: Hey, Paula, when is a storm cloud not fully dressed?
PAULA: When it's only wearing thunder wear?

(Burton, Paula, and Steve laugh; Janice rolls her eyes.)

JANICE: You are *so* immature!
STEVE: Knock-Knock!
BURTON: Who's there?
STEVE: Duane!
BURTON: Duane who?
STEVE: Shut the window, Du-ane is coming in!

(Burton, Paula, and Steve laugh; Janice watches sky, above left.)

(SOUND AND WIND EFFECTS: Wind begins gusting across stage and wind noise increases; Burton's hat blows off.)

BURTON: Whoa! That's a big wind!
STEVE: Knock, knock!
PAULA: Who's there?
STEVE: Wendy!
PAULA: Wendy who?
STEVE: *(singing)* Wen-dy wind blows, the cwadle will wock!

(Burton, Paula, and Steve laugh; Janice backs up, turns, and runs offstage right.)

JANICE: Look out! It's coming closer!

STEVE: So's Christmas!
JANICE: Run!
BURTON: Huh?

(LIGHTS FLICKER ON AND OFF; SOUND EFFECT: loud lightning and thunder, wind gusting; WIND EFFECT: wind gusts across stage; Burton, Paula, and Steve fall to ground and cover heads; EFFECTS CONTINUE FOR FIVE SECONDS, STOP; LIGHTS OUT FOR THREE SECONDS, THEN UP; FRONT SCRIM OR CURTAIN RISES revealing the town street set: a wooden sign reading "Today's Special Flavor" is on ground in front of soda shop, a motor scooter is upended at base of sign pole, crumpled magazines and newspapers are scattered in front of magazine stand.)

(MRS. BROWN dashes onstages from left as Burton, Paula, and Steve slowly get up.)

MRS. BROWN: Kids, are you all right?
PAULA: I think so, mom.
STEVE: Is my head on straight?
BURTON: Mrs. Brown, I'm hungry!
MRS. BROWN: A big wind storm just blew through the center of town. There has been a lot of damage. Say, wasn't Janice coming with you?

(Burton, Paula, and Steve look around.)

STEVE: *(points right)* She took off that way just before the storm hit.
PAULA: We thought she was just playing around.
BURTON: There she is!

(Janice enters from right, her hair disheveled; Mrs. Brown runs to her.)

MRS. BROWN: Janice, are you all right?
JANICE: Yes, Mrs. Brown. I'm fine. Just a little shaken up.
PAULA: What happened to you?

(As Janice talks, Mrs. Brown takes a notebook and pen from her purse and writes as Burton, Paula, and Steve crowd around Janice and listen.)

JANICE: Well...*(inhales, exhales deeply)* I looked up in the sky and saw this big black cloud coming our way.
STEVE: Which way did it come from?
JANICE: *(points left)* That way. Isn't that north?
MRS. BROWN: It is north, Janice.
JANICE: I tried to find some shelter and ran to get under that awning in front of the drugstore. But just when I got there, the wind ripped the awning right off the building!
BURTON: Wow!
PAULA: What happened to the awning?
JANICE: It sailed off into the wind!
STEVE: You're lucky the wind didn't pick up *you* with the awning.
PAULA: Were you scared?
JANICE: Scared? I don't think so. It all happened so fast, I didn't have time to be scared. Gee, Mrs. Brown, do we still get to watch you work?
MRS. BROWN: I'm working right now, Janice. *(waves notebook)* While you were telling us your story, and being interviewed by the other kids, I was taking notes for my story on the big storm.
JANICE: But I wasn't saying anything important
MRS. BROWN: Oh, but you were. You told us the "Four W's"

that make up the basis of every good news article: the Who, What, When, and Where. That's the first thing I learned in journalism school. Now, let's go and get the scoop on the big storm.

(MS. CALESCU enters from left and begins picking up the crumpled magazines and newspapers in front of the magazine stand.)

STEVE: *(points to Ms. Calescu)* There's Ms. Calescu. Her magazine stand sure got trashed!

(Mrs. Brown crosses to the magazine stand, followed by the kids.)

MRS. BROWN: Can we give you a hand?
MS. CALESCU: Yes, that would be wonderful. Just stack them in a pile over there. Thank you.
MRS. BROWN: No problem. I'm Judy Brown from the *Tribune*. Can you tell me what happened here? *(readies pen and notebook)*

(Kids watch the interview as they pick up magazines; Mrs. Brown writes Ms. Calescu's responses in her notebook.)

MS. CALESCU: I had just sold a magazine to a customer, Mr. Phan, when the walls started shaking. I thought the stand was going to collapse on my head!
MRS. BROWN: What did you do?
MS. CALESCU: I ducked and hit the ground! There wasn't anything else *to* do!
MRS. BROWN: That's awful. What time did the storm hit?

MS. CALESCU: Let me see. I had just looked at the clock. It must have been almost three-thirty. Maybe a little after.
MRS. BROWN: Thank you. Oh, do you remember what magazine you sold to Mr. Phan?
MS. CALESCU: Ummm, yes, it was *Model Railroading Monthly.*

(Kids finish picking up magazines; MR. TAPINSZKI enters from right and pokes around debris in front of the soda shop.)

MRS. BROWN: We'd better get going. Thanks for your time. And what is your first name, Ms. Calescu?
MS. CALESCU: Delia.
MRS. BROWN: D-E-L-I-A?
MS. CALESCU: That's right. And the name of my store is Main Street Magazines. Been here since 1994. Never seen a storm like this!
MRS. BROWN: I've got it. Thank you.
MS. CALESCU: Thank *you* folks for helping me!

(Kids wave good-bye; Mrs. Brown crosses to the soda shop, followed by the kids; Mr. Tapinszki is struggling to pick up the "Today's Special Flavor" sign.)

PAULA: Golly, look at the soda shop!
BURTON: The whole front is smashed in!
MRS. BROWN: Hello there. I'm Judy Brown from the *Tribune.*

(Kids watch the interview as Mrs. Brown writes Mr. Tapinszki's responses in her notebook.)

MR. TAPINSZKI: I'm Mel Tapinszki. Boy, this is some mess!
MRS. BROWN: Are you the owner?

MR. TAPINSZKI: No, just the day shift manager.

MRS. BROWN: Where were you when the storm hit?

MR. TAPINSZKI: I was in the back of the shop mixing up a fresh batch of strawberry-lemon tasty-whip, when I heard this big noise — like a freight train!

MRS. BROWN: Do you recall what time that was?

MR. TAPINSZKI: It was three thirty-five on the button. I was listening to the radio.

MRS. BROWN: Did you have any customers in the shop?

MR. TAPINSZKI: No, and it's lucky we didn't. They might have been hurt by broken glass.

MRS. BROWN: How do you spell your last name, Mr. Tapinszki?

MR. TAPINSZKI: Just like it sounds. T-A-P-...I-N-S-...Z-K-I.

MRS. BROWN: Thank you.

(BOBBY enters from left, carrying a motorcycle helmet; he crosses to the pole at mid center.)

JANICE: Look at that sign pole! The wind tore the sign right off it!

(Mrs. Brown crosses to the pole, followed by the kids; Bobby is staring at the upended motor scooter and shaking his head in dismay.)

MRS. BROWN: Is this your motor scooter?

BOBBY: It *was*! Now, it's a big scrap of used metal!

MRS. BROWN: I'm Judy Brown from the *Tribune*. What happened?

(Kids watch the interview as Mrs. Brown writes Bobby's responses in her notebook.)

BOBBY: I was heading up Fifth Street, when this huge gust of wind came up behind me. Pow! Next thing I know, I'm flying through the air! I landed in a flower bed, but my scooter was nowhere to be seen.

MRS. BROWN: That's incredible! Are you saying the wind carried your scooter all the way to Main Street?

BOBBY: I guess so. How else would it have gotten here?

(SHEILA BRETKOFF enters from left, followed by OFFICER D. RAU.)

SHEILA BRETKOFF: *(points at Bobby)* There he is, officer! That's the man!

(Bobby looks right to see if he can slip away, but his path is blocked by the kids. Sheila Bretkoff and Officer D. Rau approach.)

SHEILA BRETKOFF: That's the man who nearly ran me down when I was crossing Fifth Street!

BOBBY: She's crazy!

JANICE: No, she's not. He said the gust of wind came up *behind* him. Fifth Street goes one way north. And the storm came from the north. If he was heading up Fifth Street the right way, the wind would have been at his *front*, not his back.

STEVE: So if he felt the wind *behind* him, it means he was going the wrong way down Fifth Street.

SHEILA BRETKOFF: He nearly ran me down, the silly speed demon!

BOBBY: You're all nuts! I didn't say the wind came from behind. I said it came from the front.

PAULA: Did not! Check your notes, mom.

MRS. BROWN: I can do better than that. *(takes a micro-cassette recorder from her outside jacket pocket)* As a backup to my note taking I always carry a tape recorder in my pocket and leave it on during the interview. If you need additional evidence, officer, I'd be happy to loan you the tape.

BOBBY: Hey, who are you, the FBI?
PAULA: She's Judy Brown from the *Tribune*. Who are you?
BOBBY: Uh, Bobby.
JANICE: Last name?
BOBBY: Boo!
JANICE: Boo?
BOBBY: Yeh, boo to you!
STEVE: We'll see who gets the last boo, Boo!
SHEILA BRETKOFF: My name is Sheila Bretkoff. I want to swear out a complaint of reckless driving.
OFFICER D. RAU: Come along with me, sir. *(takes him by the arm)*
BURTON: *(looks at Officer D. Rau's badge-plate)* And your first name, Officer Rau?
OFFICER D. RAU: D.
STEVE: Right. And the D stands for—?
OFFICER D. RAU: D. As in D. Period.

(Burton and Steve exchange somber glances, then back away.)

STEVE & BURTON: Anything you say, officer.

(Officer D. Rau leads Bobby offstage left, with Sheila Bretkoff following.)

JANICE: That sure was exciting, Mrs. Brown. What do we do now?
MRS. BROWN: I've got to go back to the newspaper office. I'll

turn in my story about the storm and add them to the stories other reporters have collected. Then, a news editor will combine the little stories into one big story. And that's what you'll read in the paper tomorrow morning.
STEVE: Say, Janice, do you know why the newspaper building is the biggest building in the world?
JANICE: No, why?
STEVE: Because it has the most stories.

(Janice grimaces and sticks out her tongue at Steve.)

PAULA: Knock, knock!
JANICE: Who's there?
PAULA: Knock!
JANICE: Knock who?
BURTON: Knock it off! Let's go back to the soda shop and get some ice cream!
MRS. BROWN: Now, that's what I call a *real* scoop!

(Everyone laughs. LIGHTS OUT.)

THE END

Roll 'em Up, Roll 'em Up!
(Pastry Chef)

If bread is the plain staff of life, then pastry represents life's yummy pinnacle of culinary indulgence — cakes, pies, cookies, icings, and fillings of every edible texture, ingredient, and confection. While jobs in large industrial bakeries are declining because of increased automation, bakers and pastry chefs are found in greater numbers than ever working for small bakeries, restaurants and hotels that serve customers interested in home-style, custom-made bread and baked goods. Pastry chefs usually begin as general helpers at local bakeries and restaurants, before learning the fine points of the craft at vocational schools and colleges. Having a discriminating sense of taste, touch, and smell is very important to a pastry chef, along with a knowledge of basic cooking and nutrition principles.

For information about careers in baking and pastry making, contact these organizations:

American Bakers Association, 1350 I Street NW, #1290, Washington, DC 20005-3305. 202/789-0300.
http://bakingmasters.com/school/ (Baking Masters On-line Baking School)
http://www.masterpastry.com/ (Master of Pastry, featuring a genuine French pastry chef)

RUNNING TIME: 15 minutes

CAST: 9 actors, minimum 3 boys (•), 2 girls (+)

+	Paula	•	Leo (Steve's Uncle), Pastry Chef
•	Burton		Dough Mixer
+	Janice		Dough Molder
•	Steve		Oven Tender
			Icing Mixer

STAGE SET: front scrim or curtain at front of stage, behind are four mid-sized tables, blending machine, molding machine, oven*

PROPS: large measuring cup, bread-shaping knife, a section of bread dough, molding tray, tray of shaped dough, cart, four small sheet cakes in trays, small bowls containing a selection of marshmallows, lollipops, and sprinkles, four icing tubes and cones filled with royal icing; Space Alien Birthday Cake (basic ten-inch round cake decorated with outer space and alien monster motifs); four forks; four small cake plates; tablecloth for dining table; several cocktail napkins; three kazoos; three noisemakers

MUSIC: "Birthday Fanfare," "Your Birthday Is a Special Day" (two versions, one in 3/4, the other in 4/4 — you choose!)

COSTUMES: Paula, Burton, Janice, and Steve wear standard grade-school attire (Spring season); Burton wears a baseball cap and Janice has a bookbag on her back; Uncle Leo and the bakery workers wear standard baker outfits — short-sleeved white shirt, white pants, and small white cloth or paper baker's hat (Uncle Leo has a taller chef's hat)

* *Note on making prop baking machines:* For absolute accuracy you can visit a commercial bakery and construct facsimiles; however, it may suffice to construct cardboard boxes that have the prop food item inside already prepared and ready to be taken out.

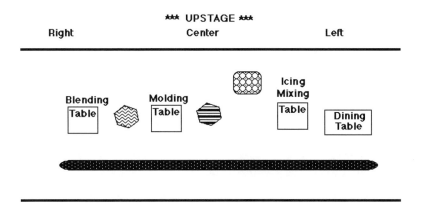

Stage Plan — *Roll 'em Up, Roll 'em Up!*

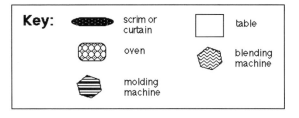

(FRONT SCRIM OR CURTAIN IS DOWN; LIGHTS UP FULL as JANICE and PAULA enter from left, STEVE and BURTON enter from right; they meet at down center.)

JANICE & PAULA:
    Pattycake, pattycake, baker man
    Bake me a cake as fast as you can!
    Roll 'em up, roll 'em up
    Put 'em in the pan!

STEVE & BURTON:
    Put 'em in the pan
    And set 'em out to rise!
    Up comes a cake
    Before your very eyes!

JANICE & PAULA:
    Roll 'em up, roll 'em up —

STEVE & BURTON:
    Roll 'em up, roll 'em up —

ALL:
    Roll 'em up, roll 'em up
    Put 'em in the pan!

UNCLE LEO: *(shouts from behind scrim)* Hey, kids! Come on in!

(SCRIM RISES revealing the inside of a commercial bakery; across the middle of the stage from right to left are (1) DOUGH MIXER standing behind a dough mixing table, (2) a blending machine, (3) DOUGH MOLDER standing behind a molding table, (4) a molding *machine, (5) OVEN TENDER standing in front of an oven, (6) an icing mixing table and (7) UNCLE LEO standing in front of a dining table.)*

UNCLE LEO: Welcome to the bakery! I'm Steve's uncle, Uncle Leo. Who are you guys?
PAULA: I'm Paula!
BURTON: I'm Burton!
JANICE: I'm Janice!
STEVE: I'm actually Steve's clone. The real Steve was too tired to be up this early.
UNCLE LEO: Always a wise guy! Say, isn't this the best place in the whole world to spend a Saturday morning? *(gestures around the bakery)* It all happens right here, kids: cakes, cookies, pies, delicious treats of every description. And don't forget the most common food in the entire world — bread!
JANICE: *(raises hand)* People in the Middle East were making bread twelve thousand years ago.
UNCLE LEO: And they still are. Who knows what Middle Eastern bread is called today?
BURTON: *(raises hand)* Pita bread!
UNCLE LEO: Bingo! How about in Mexico?
PAULA: *(raises hand)* Tortillas!
UNCLE LEO: Ireland?
BURTON: *(raises hand)* Soda bread!
UNCLE LEO: France?
STEVE: *(raises hand)* Baguettes!
UNCLE LEO: India?
JANICE: *(raises hand)* Chapatis!
UNCLE LEO: Rightarooni! It's a big wide world of bread, kids. Everybody wants it, and we make our own special recipe of American-style bread right here in the bakery. Let's see how it works.

(Uncle Leo crosses to dough mixing table at mid right; kids follow and stand between Uncle Leo and mid center.)

UNCLE LEO: Who knows what bread is made from?

BURTON: *(raises hand)* Flour?

UNCLE LEO: Flour! And I don't mean petunias! Flour F-L-O-U-R flour made from the kernels of grains like wheat, oats, corn, rye, millet, and barley. The kernels get ground up at the mill into flour. When the flour comes to us from the mill, it goes to the Dough Mixer.

DOUGH MIXER: *(holds up large measuring cup)* I mix flour, water, and salt together in that big blending machine. *(points to blending machine)* I have to weigh all the ingredients very carefully. Then I add yeast.

JANICE: *(raises hand)* Yeast is a tiny living plant.

DOUGH MIXER: And when yeast is mixed into bread dough, it feeds on the sugar and starch in the dough. The yeast makes the bread dough rise to twice its original size.

UNCLE LEO: Then we take the dough to the Dough Molder.

(Dough Molder takes a section of dough from the mixing machine and places it on a tray on the molding table.)

DOUGH MOLDER: I mold the dough into whatever shape and size I want — rolling it around in my hands, squeezing it, cutting it with a big knife, like so. *(kneads and shapes and cuts dough)* Then it goes back on the shelf to rise some more.

UNCLE LEO: Until it's really nice and puffy and almost ready for the oven.

(DOUGH MOLDER takes the tray of dough and puts it in the molding machine.)

DOUGH MOLDER: Sometimes we use the molding machine to do the job.

(OVEN TENDER takes the tray of shaped dough from the molding machine and displays it.)

OVEN TENDER: Then the Oven Tender — that's me — sticks the dough into the hot, *hot* oven.
UNCLE LEO: Very, very *very* hot oven!
JANICE: How hot?
OVEN TENDER: About four hundred degrees hot!
BURTON, PAULA, JANICE, & STEVE: That's *hot!*
OVEN TENDER: When the bread is baked, it comes out of the oven and is loaded onto cooling trays —
UNCLE LEO: Where I, the master baker, inspect the loaves and give my master baker seal of approval.

(Dough Mixer, Dough Molder, and Oven Tender exit right as ICING MIXER enters from left, pulling behind a cart containing cake decorating materials, and stands at military-style attention at down left.)

STEVE: *(raises hand)* Uncle Leo?
UNCLE LEO: Yes?
STEVE: *(points to Icing Mixer)* Who is that?
UNCLE LEO: Ah-ha! Just in the nick of time! Ladies and gentlemen, allow me to introduce every pastry chef's secret weapon — the Icing Mixer!

(Icing Mixer bows and pulls cart to mixing table as kids and Uncle Leo applaud.)

ICING MIXER: My job is to mix up the icing that makes pastry appeal to your eyes as well as your taste buds. This morning, I've mixed up a batch you can try out for yourselves.

(Kids shout all at once.)

BURTON: All right!
PAULA: Neato!
STEVE: Yeh!
JANICE: Cool!

(Kids stand behind icing mixing table as Uncle Leo and Icing Mixer distribute the decorating materials — a small sheet cake in front of each kid; small bowls containing marshmallows, lollipops, and sprinkles — on the icing table; four icing tubes and cones filled with royal icing. Kids dig in and start decorating the cakes under Uncle Leo's encouraging supervision as Icing Mixer quietly spreads tablecloth and napkins on dining table.)

UNCLE LEO: That's the ticket!
BURTON: This is really fun!
UNCLE LEO: Very good, very good!
PAULA: I'm making a bird!
UNCLE LEO: Muy excellente, amigo! Muy excellente!
JANICE: I'm making an airplane!
UNCLE LEO: You kids are sensational!
STEVE: I'm making a bird and airplane crash landing! Splat!

(MUSIC: Dough Mixer, Dough Molder, and Oven Tender play "Birthday Fanfare" on kazoos offstage left.)

UNCLE LEO: Hark! What yonder trumpets sound?
(Oven Tender marches out from right holding a finished

birthday cake, followed by Dough Mixer holding four forks and Dough Molder holding four cake plates; they cross to dining table and put cake, forks and plates on dining table.)

STEVE: What's going on, Uncle Leo? Is today somebody's birthday?

UNCLE LEO: *Every* day is *some*body's birthday! But today just happens to be the birthday…of my nephew Steve!

BURTON, PAULA, & JANICE: Surprise! *(they take noisemakers from their pockets and blow at the astonished Steve)*

STEVE: It *is* my birthday! I can't believe you guys remembered!

PAULA: How could we forget? You've been bugging everybody at school for the last month.

BURTON: Look, it's a Space Alien Birthday Cake!

STEVE: With space ships and monsters!

PAULA: The three-eyed one is oozing green stuff!

JANICE: Eewww, gross!

UNCLE LEO: Dig in, kids! It's a masterpiece made for eating!

STEVE: Uncle Leo, you were right. This is the best place in the whole world to spend a Saturday morning!

(Dough Mixer, Dough Molder, Oven Tender and Icing Mixer sing "Your Birthday Is a Special Day.")

DOUGH MIXER, DOUGH MOLDER, OVEN TENDER, & ICING MIXER: *(sing)*
Your birthday is a very special day
Full of fun and friends and so many games to play.
We wish you lots of happiness and cheer
Because your birthday is the best day of the year.

UNCLE LEO: *(to audience)* Come on now, it's going to be your birthday one of these days. Everybody sing!

ENTIRE CAST: *(sings)*
　　Your birthday is a very special day
　　Full of fun and friends and so many games to play.
　　We wish you lots of happiness and cheer
　　Because your birthday is the best day of the year.
　　Because your birthday is the best day of the year.

(Everyone applauds. LIGHTS OUT.)

THE END

Your Birthday Is a Very Special Day (#1)
(words & music by L.E. McCullough)

© L.E. McCullough 1998

[last time through tune, repeat final phrase as tag:
"because your birthday is the best day of the year"]

Your Birthday Is a Very Special Day (#2)
(words & music by L.E. McCullough)

© L.E. McCullough 1998

[last time through tune, repeat final phrase as tag:
"because your birthday is the best day of the year"]

Birthday Fanfare
(by L.E. McCullough)

© L.E. McCullough 1998

Call of the Wild
(Park Ranger)

Park rangers are employed by state and federal governments to help preserve and protect the natural resources of our public parks. Park rangers prevent forest fires, rescue lost and injured hikers, protect wildlife, and make sure that people visiting parks abide by the rules. They also often teach courses about nature and wildlife to park visitors. In college, park rangers study botany, geology, zoology, forestry, and various forms of environmental science in order to know as much about nature as possible. If you are interested in a career as a park ranger, you can start by volunteering as a park aide at your local city, state, or national park.

For information about a career as a park ranger, contact these organizations:

National Recreation and Park Association, 2775 S. Quincy Street, #300, Alexandria, VA 22206-2204. 703/820-4940.
http://www.dnr.state.wi.us/org/caer/ce/eek/index.htm (Wisconsin Dept. of Natural Resources, which includes "Diary of a Park Ranger")
http://www.for.nau.edu/prm/rangers/Default.htm (Northern Arizona University School of Forestry's Park Ranger Training Program)

RUNNING TIME: 15 minutes

CAST: 14 actors, minimum 6 boys (•), 5 girls (+)

+	Paula	+	Gina Boyd, Park Ranger
•	Burton	+	Fisherman
+	Janice	+/•	2 Hikers
•	Steve		3 Picnickers
•	Mr. Brooks, Teacher	•	Bird Watcher
		•	Glen, Park Volunteer

STAGE SET: picnic table at down left; large stone or boulder at down right; tree at mid center; entrances at down right and up right, down left and up left

PROPS: fishing rod, gum stick wrapper, toy bird (robin), binoculars, butterfly net, notebook, pen, picnic blanket, picnic basket, sandwiches, hiking stick, trail map, cell phone, towel, hiking boot, popsicle stick, small plastic bag

EFFECTS: Sound — marsh and woodland sounds; chirping baby bird; cell phone ringing; bear cub growling

COSTUMES: Paula, Burton, Janice, and Steve wear standard grade-school attire (Spring season) with outdoor walking shoes and jackets; Burton wears a baseball cap and Janice has a bookbag on her back; Mr. Brooks wears a standard male teacher's school outfit with a windbreaker or outdoors jacket; Gina Boyd wears a park ranger uniform — brown or black hiking boots, brown shirt, khaki or dark green pants and jacket with a metal badge on the jacket front and a patch reading "Park Ranger" sewn on the right shoulder of the jacket; Glen the Park Volunteer wears the same park ranger uniform as Gina Boyd but without the metal badge or Park Ranger patch; Fisherman, Hikers, Picnickers, and Bird Watcher wear outdoor leisure clothes with Fisherman having a pair of wading boots and the Hikers wearing hiking boots

Right	**★★ UPSTAGE ★★** Center	Left

Stage Plan — *Call of the Wild*

Key: tree, boulder, picnic table

(LIGHTS UP FULL on MR. BROOKS, JANICE, PAULA, BURTON, and STEVE standing by and/or sitting at the picnic table at down left.)

MR. BROOKS: Well, class, this is Tahtokah State Park. Fourteen hundred acres of beautiful hills, woods, creeks, and lakes — and only a few miles from our city limits. How many have been to the park before?

(Janice, Paula, Burton, and Steve raise their hands.)

JANICE: My family goes sailing here every summer.
PAULA: We came to a Fourth of July cookout last year.

STEVE: I went sledding with my church group on Christmas Eve.

BURTON: My dad and I fished in the creek once. I caught a worm.

MR. BROOKS: Then you know there are a lot of fun things to do in this park. Here comes our guide now to tell us more.

(GINA BOYD, PARK RANGER, enters from left.)

MR. BROOKS: Hello, I am Mr. Brooks, and this is our field trip class. Thank you for having us today.

GINA BOYD: You are very welcome. My name is Gina Boyd. I am a park ranger here at Tahtokah State Park. Does anyone know how the park got its name?

JANICE: *(raises hand)* Isn't Tahtokah a Native American word?

GINA BOYD: Yes, it is. Tahtokah means *antelope* in the Sioux language. There once were many Indian tribes who lived here, and the name of the park preserves their memory.

PAULA: *(raises hand)* Are there still lots of antelope in the park?

GINA BOYD: Not any more. Antelopes have to live very far away from people. And as you can see, a state park is very popular place with many people. *(points to THREE PICNICKERS entering from up right and spreading blanket at mid center)*

BURTON: Look, they're having a picnic!

GINA BOYD: Many families come to the park, just to relax in a quiet, peaceful place. And some people, like that fisherman on the edge of the creek, *(points down right at FISHERMAN with fishing rod leaning against boulder, casting his line offstage right)* come to the park to work a little bit and see if they can't catch their dinner.

(TWO HIKERS enter from up left and cross stage briskly to exit down right; one carries a hiking stick, the other an unfolded trail map.)

STEVE: There go some hikers!
GINA BOYD: Lots of people come to walk the trails that go through the woods. It is very good exercise.
MR. BROOKS: What is your favorite thing to do in the park, Ranger Boyd?
GINA BOYD: I like to take nature hikes and visit the animals who make the park their permanent home all year round. Come on, I'll show you! Be very quiet, and you can hear the animals talk!

(Gina Boyd leads the Class with Mr. Brooks bringing up the rear across stage to down right; as they walk, the Fisherman exits right, the Picnickers exit up right. SOUND EFFECT: marsh and woodland sounds. At down right, Gina Boyd sits on boulder and addresses the Class.)

GINA BOYD: Did you hear any animals talking when we walked by the edge of the lake?
CLASS: *(nodding assent)* Mmm-hmm.
GINA BOYD: Did you see any animals?
JANICE: *(raises hand)* I saw ducks!
PAULA: *(raises hand)* I saw geese!
STEVE: *(raises hand)* I saw a turtle!
BURTON: *(raises hand)* I saw a frog being eaten by a snake!
JANICE & PAULA: Ewwwww!

GINA BOYD: *(points offstage right into audience)* Look, there's a deer! Shhh!

(Mr. Brooks and Class follow Gina Boyd's gaze; a BIRD WATCHER enters from left with binoculars around his neck and stands at down left looking up in the sky; he absentmindedly unwraps a gum stick and drops the wrapper on the ground, and Gina Boyd notices.)

PAULA: Gosh, Ranger Boyd, being a park ranger sure is a lot of fun!

GINA BOYD: Yes, it is. But sometimes it is very serious — when we have to remind people about the park rules.

(Gina Boyd addresses Bird Watcher and walks purposefully to down center.)

GINA BOYD: Sir!

BIRD WATCHER: Are you talking to me?

GINA BOYD: Sir, my name is Park Ranger Gina Boyd. I noticed that you dropped a piece of paper in the grass.

BIRD WATCHER: Huh? *(looks down)* Oh, yeh. Sorry. *(picks up wrapper, puts it in his pocket and resumes bird watching, before exiting left)*

GINA BOYD: Thank you, sir. Have a nice day!

MR. BROOKS: Do you have a lot of park rules, Ranger Boyd?

GINA BOYD: Just enough so we can protect the park and keep it clean and safe for the animals who live here and the people who come to visit. A big part of my job is reminding people to do what they know they *should* do.

(SOUND EFFECT: chirping baby bird.)

GINA BOYD: Listen! Do you hear that sound?

(Everyone listens intently, as Gina Boyd walks slowly toward mid center.)

JANICE: It sounds like a bird.
BURTON: Is it a baby bird calling for its parents?
STEVE: Where is it?
PAULA: I think it's over there!
GINA BOYD: Here it is!

(Gina Boyd bends down in front of tree and picks up injured bird; Class gathers around; SOUND EFFECT: Chirping baby bird sounds continue until Gina Boyd finishes phone call.)

MR. BROOKS: It looks like a baby robin.
GINA BOYD: It is a baby robin. It must have fallen from its nest.
JANICE: Is it hurt?
GINA BOYD: I think its right wing is bent.
STEVE: Awwww…
JANICE: Oooh, it's in pain!
BURTON: I bet it gets eaten by a snake!
PAULA: You can't leave it here!
GINA BOYD: *(pulls cell phone from her jacket and speaks into phone)* Hello? This is Ranger Boyd. I'm at Marker Eighteen on Trail Number Seven. We have found an injured bird. Can you send a volunteer to bring the bird into the aid station? Thank you! *(disconnects phone)* We will do the best we can to help this baby bird get well.
STEVE: Gee whiz, a park ranger has to be part policeman, part teacher, and part doctor!
GINA BOYD: It all adds up to one thing — a park ranger must preserve the natural resources we all depend upon.

(GLEN, a volunteer, rushes onstage from right, carrying a towel.)

GLEN: Hello. My name is Glen, a park volunteer. I will take the injured bird in for treatment.
GINA BOYD: Thank you. *(puts bird on Glen's towel)*

(Glen exits right; SOUND EFFECT: cell phone ringing.)

GINA BOYD: *(answers phone)* Ranger Boyd. What? Oh no, that sounds very bad! I am on my way right now! *(disconnects phone)*
MR. BROOKS: What is the problem, Ranger Boyd? Another injured animal?
GINA BOYD: No. Someone reported their friends are lost and may be in trouble. We had better hurry!

(Gina Boyd leads Class to up left; she stops and looks around.)

GINA BOYD: We are looking for a young man and woman, around age twenty. They were last seen heading up this trail.

(Burton spies a popsicle stick on the ground.)

BURTON: Look! A popsicle stick!

(Gina Boyd picks up the popsicle stick and studies it.)

GINA BOYD: You have very sharp eyes. It is still moist. If this belonged to the hikers, they were here not long ago.
JANICE: I will put that in my litter bag, Ranger Boyd. *(puts stick in small plastic bag)*

GINA BOYD: Thank you. That is planning ahead!

(Gina Boyd leads Class to down left; she stops and looks at picnic table and points.)

GINA BOYD: What is that on the table?
PAULA: *(picks up unfolded trail map)* It is a trail map.
STEVE: I bet it belonged to those hikers we saw back at the ranger station!
GINA BOYD: They should not have gone hiking in these woods without their map. I wonder why they left it here?

(Gina Boyd leads Class to mid center; Steve points to tree.)

STEVE: Over there!

(Burton runs to tree, picks up hiking boot, and holds it aloft.)

PAULA: A hiking boot!
GINA BOYD: This is not a good sign. Something must have scared the person who lost this. *(sniffs)* Something very furry…and very hungry…

(Two Hikers enter from right and crouch, terrified, on top of boulder [Hiker #1 has no boot]; they look offstage right and shout.)

HIKER #1: Help! Help!
HIKER #2: Get away, get away, get away! Shoo!

(SOUND EFFECT: bear cub growling. Gina Boyd and Class turn and look down right.)

GINA BOYD: They are down by the ravine! A family of bears was spotted there last week!
STEVE: Uh-ohhhhh...Fresh hiker nuggets!

(Hikers continue to crouch on boulder and shout toward offstage right as Gina Boyd leads Class to down right; SOUND EFFECT: Bear cub growling subsides.)

HIKER #1: Andale! Andale!
HIKER #2: *Andale?* Does the bear speak Spanish!
HIKER #1: Who knows? He might! Andale!
HIKER #2: Andale! Andale!
GINA BOYD: Hallo! It is all right! The bear has gone away!
HIKER #1: We are safe!
HIKER #2: Thank goodness! We got off the trail a ways back and were crossing the ravine. The next thing we knew, we heard this horrible growling!
HIKER #1: And this huge monstrous bear came bounding out of the woods!
HIKER #2: He was mean!
HIKER #1: He was vicious!
HIKER #2: He was totally psycho!
GINA BOYD: Judging from the paw prints in the mud, he was a cub about three months old. He probably smelled the food you have been littering the trail with for the last few miles. Didn't you see the signs at the park entrance? Do *not* litter and do *not* feed the animals!
HIKER #1: Sure, *we* saw the signs...
HIKER #2: But who knew that *bears* could read?
GINA BOYD: You had better follow us back to the ranger station. And we can go over the park rules in detail.
HIKERS #1 & 2: Yes, Ranger!

(Two Hikers sit on rock and tie their boots; Burton hands the missing boot to Hiker #1.)

MR. BROOKS: That is a good example of how important it is to know the rules of the park.

GINA BOYD: And to follow them. These hikers were very, very lucky they did not get hurt.

JANICE: I guess that being in a state park is like visiting somebody's house. You have to treat everything with respect.

PAULA: And not act like nature belongs only to you.

STEVE: Or else there won't be any part of nature left to enjoy.

BURTON: Including you! *(growls like a bear at Two Hikers who startle and jump)*

(LIGHTS OUT.)

THE END

Opening Night at the Opera, er, Opry
(Piano Tuner)

Piano tuners not only have to be able to twist a few piano strings, they often have to rebuild parts of a piano's inside and outside to get it sounding right. And whether it sounds "right" is often a matter of differing opinion to every set of listening ears! A capable piano tuner knows as much about woodworking and metalcraft as she knows about music and is as familiar with a hammer and gluegun as with a pitch pipe. While many piano tuners and technicians work for music stores, piano and keyboard manufacturers, and concert halls, a growing number are self-employed and take care of pianos in schools and private homes. After completing a formal course of study in piano tuning and repair, you will want to hire on as an apprentice to a more experienced piano technician. Experts agree: No two pianos are the same!

For information about a career as a piano tuner and technician, contact these organizations:

Piano Technicians Guild, 3930 Washington, Kansas City, MO 64111. 816/753-7747.

http://www.piano-tuning.com/ (American School of Piano Tuning)

http://www.tiac.net/users/pianos/pianotuningschools.htm (a list of piano tuning schools throughout the world)

And, since opera and country singers are mentioned in the play, check out these web sites as well:

http://www.metguild.org/ (Metropolitan Opera Guild)

http://www.country.com/home.html (Country Music, including the Grand Ole Opry)

RUNNING TIME: 20 minutes

CAST: 9 actors, minimum 4 boys (•), 5 girls (+)

+	Paula	+	Brenda Foy, Piano Tuner
•	Burton	•	Herman, the Hall Manager
+	Janice	+	Madame Fifi, Classical Soprano
•	Steve	+	Dolly Mae Cottonwood, Country Singer
•	Mr. Brooks, Teacher		

STAGE SET: a grand or baby grand piano with bench stands at down center (if no real piano is available, try making a facsimile real-size cardboard piano and have the piano notes sound from a tape player offstage)

PROPS: guitar, contract, handkerchief, piano tuning tools: tuning hammer, two rubber mutes, tuning fork, pitch pipe

MUSIC: *Them Old Tuna Fields Back Home*

COSTUMES: Paula, Burton, Janice, and Steve wear standard grade-school attire (Spring season); Burton wears a baseball cap and Janice has a bookbag on her back; Mr. Brooks wears a standard male teacher's school outfit; Brenda Foy wears casual blouse and slacks and flat shoes; Hall Manager wears a three-piece business suit; Dolly Mae Cottonwood wears a country-western stage outfit: cowboy hat, rhinestone-studded western shirt and jeans, boots; Madame Fifi is attired in a formal evening or ballroom gown and heels

Stage Plan — *Opening Night at the Opera, er, Opry*

Key: piano   bench

Actor Positions:

1 Brenda Foy   6 Burton
2 Mr. Brooks   7 Hall Manager
3 Steve   8 Madame Fifi
4 Janice   9 Dolly Mae
5 Paula

(STAGE IS DARK; a piano is being tuned, and middle C is plunked several times. Offstage, a female soprano does a vocal exercise. LIGHTS UP FULL on MR. BROOKS entering from right and leading JANICE, PAULA, BURTON, and STEVE to down center where BRENDA FOY, PIANO TUNER, is tuning a grand piano; the piano has its top lid open facing out toward the audience and several tuning tools lie on the bench. Vocalizing fades as dialogue begins.)

BRENDA FOY: Hello! You must be Mr. Brooks and his class. My name is Brenda Foy, and I am the resident piano tuner here at the concert hall.

MR. BROOKS: Thanks for letting us stop by. We know you're busy tuning for a big concert tonight. Just keep working and let us watch.

BRENDA FOY: All right. Who knows how many notes a piano has?

STEVE: Eighty-eight?

BRENDA FOY: That's right, white keys and black keys together. And each time you press a key on the keyboard, you get a note. The lowest note starts on the left of the keyboard, and the notes get higher as you keep moving to the right. Why don't we take a look at the inside?

(Class gathers around piano and peers under the lid.)

PAULA: Gee, it looks like a big harp lying on its side!

BRENDA FOY: It certainly does. The piano strings are streched across a wooden frame. When a player presses a key on the keyboard, that moves a jack inside the piano that is connected to a hammer, which is a felt-covered piece of wood that strikes the string and makes the sound we hear. *(presses a key to illustrate)*

JANICE: *(raises hand)* How come some of the notes hit more than one string?

BRENDA FOY: That's very observant. On this piano, nine of the lowest notes are sounded by one string. The next sixteen notes above them have two strings each. And all the rest of the notes above them have three strings per note.

STEVE: You have to tune *all* those strings?

BRENDA FOY: Yes, I do. And each group of strings on a particular note has to be tuned perfectly in unison with one another.

BURTON: You must have incredible hearing!

BRENDA FOY: I have a good sense of musical pitch. But I

can't depend on that alone. To be completely accurate, I have this tool to help me.

(Brenda Foy takes a tuning fork from the bench and holds it aloft.)

BRENDA FOY: This object is called a tuning fork. It is made of hard steel and made to sound one note when you strike it against a hard surface — like this.

(She strikes tuning fork on her wrist, then holds the base on the top edge of the piano allowing it to vibrate audibly.)

PAULA: Wow!
JANICE: Neat!
STEVE: Co-ool!
BURTON: I know that note! It's the note our vacuum cleaner makes when it's swallowed a nail!
BRENDA FOY: My goodness! You must have perfect pitch. That was an A note, and it should match this note on the piano. *(plays an A above middle C)* Pretty close!

(Brenda Foy takes a pitch pipe from the bench and gives it to Burton.)

BRENDA FOY: Go ahead and blow!

(Burton blows a note.)

BRENDA FOY: That is my pitch pipe. Each note is tuned to a standard pitch in the musical scale. When I come to a D on the piano, for instance, I can blow a D on the pitch pipe and know what the piano note is supposed to sound like.

(Burton puts the pitch pipe back on the bench, as Brenda Foy takes a tuning hammer and two mutes from from the bench.)

JANICE: *(raises hand)* How do you make the strings get back in tune?

BRENDA FOY: This is a tuning hammer. It turns the tuning pins that hold the strings to the frame. Like so. *(turns a pin inside the piano while plucking the string with finger)* Hear the pitch change?

PAULA: The pitch got higher.

BRENDA FOY: That's because I made the string tighter and shorter.

BURTON: What do you use those wedge-shaped things for?

BRENDA FOY: These are mutes. I stick them in between strings so the strings won't sound. That way, when I'm concentrating on tuning one note, I won't get distracted by other sounds. *(sticks mutes in between strings)* Tuning a piano is simple. You just have to be very careful and precise, because the artists who play the piano want to sound their best at all times.

(DOLLY MAE COTTONWOOD enters from left, holding a guitar, and stands at down left staring at group gathered at piano.)

MR. BROOKS: Who are you tuning the piano for tonight?

BRENDA FOY: According to my schedule, this piano is going to accompany a classical singer, Madame Fifi.

(Dolly Mae Cottonwood twangs a dissonant guitar chord.)

DOLLY MAE COTTONWOOD: You better check your calendar, missy!

(Dolly Mae Cottonwood marches to down center.)

DOLLY MAE COTTONWOOD: Howdy.

(The others stare at her but say nothing.)

DOLLY MAE COTTONWOOD: I said, "Howdy!"
BRENDA FOY, MR. BROOKS, JANICE, PAULA, BURTON, & STEVE: Howdy!
DOLLY MAE COTTONWOOD: That's more friendly-like. My name is Dolly Mae Cottonwood, and *I* will be this pi-ana's singing partner tonight!
BRENDA FOY: But I thought Madame Fifi was giving a concert of classical music?
DOLLY MAE COTTONWOOD: Honey, are you paid to think or tune pi-anas? No Madame Fluffy is gonna hogtie my stage!

(Dolly Mae Cottonwood sings "Them Old Tuna Fields Back Home," off-pitch and thrashing the guitar.)

DOLLY MAE COTTONWOOD: *(sings)*
When I was a little bitty baby
My mama would knock me with a ladle
In them old tuna fields back home!

(While Dolly Mae Cottonwood sings, MADAME FIFI enters from right followed by HALL MANAGER; they stand at down right and watch Dolly Mae Cottonwood sing, Madame Fifi frowning with hands on her hips, the

Hall Manager cringing and holding his hands over his ears.)

MADAME FIFI: *(to Hall Manager)* Herman, you are the Hall Manager, is that not correct?

HALL MANAGER: Yes, Madame Fifi, I am the Hall Manager, yes, yes…*(waves at Class)* hello, there, hi…

MADAME FIFI: Then, I have but one simple, straightforward question: Who is this creature, and why is she standing at *my* piano making that horrid, horrid noise?

DOLLY MAE COTTONWOOD: *Your* pi-ana? I don't see your name branded on the side!

MADAME FIFI: As if *you* could *read*!

DOLLY MAE COTTONWOOD: *(reaches behind her and takes a contract from her belt, brandishing it defiantly)* I can read this booking contract, and it says that I, Dolly Mae Cottonwood, are the sole performer in this the-ater tonight!

(Madame Fifi strides to down center, timidly followed by Hall Manager.)

MADAME FIFI: May I see the contract?

(Hall Manager crosses to Dolly Mae Cottonwood, takes the contract, and gives it to Madame Fifi. Without so much as a glance at its contents, Madame Fifi calmly rips it in half and wads up both halves, placing them in the outstretched hands of the Hall Manager.)

MADAME FIFI: I think we've solved *that* problem!

HALL MANAGER: Now, ladies, it would seem that we, uh, perhaps *I* made a slight error and booked the hall to *both* of you — on the same night.

MADAME FIFI & DOLLY MAE COTTONWOOD: You what?
HALL MANAGER: I'm certain we can work something out.
DOLLY MAE COTTONWOOD: Darn tootin'! You can work *her* right out the door!
MADAME FIFI: How dare you speak that way to Madame Fifi, the toast of Europe!
DOLLY MAE COTTONWOOD: You could be the peanut butter and jelly sandwich of Kalamazoo for all I care! It's *my* show tonight!
MADAME FIFI: Is not!
DOLLY MAE COTTONWOOD: Is!
MADAME FIFI: Not!
DOLLY MAE COTTONWOOD: Is!
MADAME FIFI: Not!
DOLLY MAE COTTONWOOD: Is!
MADAME FIFI: *(sings loudly)* Not!
DOLLY MAE COTTONWOOD: Is! *(strums guitar)*
MADAME FIFI: *(sings loudly)* Not!
DOLLY MAE COTTONWOOD: Is! *(strums guitar)*
MADAME FIFI: *(sings loudly as Dolly Mae Cottonwood strums guitar)* Not! Na-na-na-na-na-na-nottttttt!
HALL MANAGER: Ladies, please!

(Silence for five seconds.)

JANICE: *(raises hand)* Why don't you take turns sharing the stage?
MADAME FIFI: I beg your pardon!
PAULA: Madame Fifi could sing for one hour and Dolly Mae could sing for another hour.
STEVE: That way you could both use the stage.
BURTON: And since your fans would be getting two concerts for one, you could charge double the price.

DOLLY MAE COTTONWOOD: These younguns may have somethin' there!

HALL MANAGER: What do you say, ladies? It's a perfect solution.

(Madame Fifi and Dolly Mae Cottonwood frown silently for five seconds.)

HALL MANAGER: There you go. Let's shake hands.

(Hall Manager takes hold of each woman by the arm and pulls them together, forcing them together in a handshake from which each woman quickly recoils — Dolly Mae rubbing her hand on her jeans and Madame Fifi wiping her hand with a handkerchief.)

HALL MANAGER: Splendid! Who needs contracts anyway when we have good old-fashioned trust?

MADAME FIFI: Which of us will sing first?

DOLLY MAE COTTONWOOD: Well, I ain't a-singin' last!

MADAME FIFI: *(sings)* I *am* the headliner, after all!

HALL MANAGER: Ladies, ladies, ladies!

(Hall Manager pulls Madame Fifi and Dolly Mae Cottonwood offstage left.)

DOLLY MAE COTTONWOOD: Oh no, I'm not gonna follow that canary!

MADAME FIFI: *(sings)* You are a croaking weasel!

HALL MANAGER: We'll work something out, let's just relax our vocal chords now...

(They exit arguing.)

MR. BROOKS: Well, class, we'd better let Ms. Foy get back to her tuning. She doesn't have much time before the concert begins.

BRENDA FOY: Thanks for dropping by. As you can see, the life of a piano tuner isn't easy...but it's never dull!

(Mr. Brooks leads Janice, Paula, Burton, and Steve offstage right, as Brenda Foy resumes tuning. As LIGHTS FADE OUT, the simultaneous sounds of Madame Fifi vocalizing and Dolly Mae Cottonwood yodeling are heard offstage left.)

MADAME FIFI: La-la-la-la-la-la-la-la-la!

DOLLY MAE COTTONWOOD: Yodel-ay-hee-hoo! Yodel-odel-odel-odel-ay-hee-hoo!

(LIGHTS OUT.)

THE END

OPENING NIGHT 55

It's an Emergency!
(Emergency Medical Technician)

The working hours of an EMT (emergency medical technician) are as stress-filled as any occupation in existence — life-and-death decisions must be made at a second's notice, often in dangerous situations. Yet, in helping to save lives and provide assistance to the sick and injured, an EMT receives tremendous satisfaction. To enter an emergency medical technician training program, you must be at least eighteen years old, have a high school diploma, and possess a valid driver's license. After approximately one hundred hours of classroom training, an aspiring EMT spends a minimum of six months working with experienced Emergency Medical Service teams on ambulance rescues. Volunteers are always welcome at EMS sites, and you can check with hospitals and police and fire departments in your area to see if they are looking for aides.

For information about a career as an emergency medical technician, contact these organizations:

National Association of Emergency Medical Technicians, 102 W. Leake Street, Clinton, MS 39056. 800/346-2368.
http://www.fire-ems.net/ (The Fire and EMS Information Network)
http://www.seas.gwu.edu/faculty/gwems/index.html (George Washington University EMS Program)

RUNNING TIME: 15 minutes

CAST: 11 actors, minimum 4 boys (•), 6 girls (+)

- + Paula
- • Burton
- • Mr. Brooks, Teacher
- + Janice
- • Steve
-   Dispatcher (offstage)
- + Barbara Nielsen, Emergency Medical Technician
- • Walter Carillo, Emergency Medical Technician
- + Mrs. Bingham, Elderly Woman
- + Myrna Brice, Passerby
- + Policewoman

STAGE SET: at down right are four chairs and a table; midway between down center and down left is a box large and strong enough for sitting; a trash can lid lies a few feet to the right and up

PROPS: trash can lid, Kleenex, a bag of groceries, medical supply bag, two pairs of disposable latex gloves, penlight, blood pressure cuff, icepack, pill bottle

EFFECTS: Sound — dispatch radio static; ambulance siren

COSTUMES: Paula, Burton, Janice, and Steve wear standard grade-school attire (Spring season); Burton wears a baseball cap and Janice has a bookbag on her back; Mr. Brooks wears a standard male teacher's school outfit; Emergency Medical Technicians wear standard EMS uniforms — dark pants, light blue shirts with an I.D. nameplate on front of shirt and a patch reading "EMS Services" sewn on right shoulder; Policewoman wears standard city police uniform; Mrs. Bingham wears floral print dress, house slippers; Myrna Brice wears casual blouse and slacks

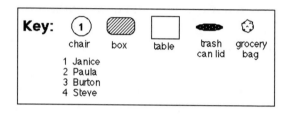

Stage Plan — *It's an Emergency!*

(LIGHTS UP RIGHT on JANICE, PAULA, BURTON, and STEVE sitting at down right around a table, flanked by BARBARA NIELSEN and WALTER CARILLO, two Emergency Medical Technicians; MR. BROOKS stands behind students.)

BARBARA NIELSEN: Good morning, students. And thank you, Mr. Brooks, for bringing the class to our EMS Dispatch Center. Welcome!

WALTER CARILLO: Who knows what EMS stands for?

JANICE: *(raises hand)* EMS stands for Emergency Medical Services.

BARBARA NIELSEN: That's right. My name is Barbara Nielsen.

WALTER CARILLO: I am Walter Carillo. We are Emergency Medical Technicians.

BARBARA NIELSEN: Our job is to provide immediate help to victims of accidents or critical illness. We work at the scene of an accident, or on the way to the hospital, or even in a hospital emergency room.

WALTER CARILLO: Very often an EMS team is the first source of medical assistance. We have to be able to figure out very quickly what is wrong with the person and how they can best be treated. If someone's life is in danger, we treat them right away.

BARBARA NIELSEN: Have any of you ever been assisted by an EMS team?

BURTON: *(raises hand)* When I was a baby, my mother thought I swallowed poison.

BARBARA NIELSEN: And did an EMS team help you?

BURTON: They came to our house and made me throw up. But it wasn't poison, just too much rhubarb pie.

WALTER CARILLO: Your mother was correct in calling EMS. If you *had* swallowed poison, it would have been very important to treat you as soon as possible.

PAULA: *(raises hand)* I saw an EMS team help a man who had a heart attack at the mall. They did something called CPR?

BARBARA NIELSEN: That's right. CPR stands for "cardiopulmonary resuscitation." That's a big long term that basically means you get someone's heart started after it has stopped.

MR. BROOKS: What other kind of skills does an Emergency Medical Technician need?

WALTER CARILLO: An Emergency Medical Technician must know how to stop and control bleeding, give oxygen to someone who has stopped breathing, and treat broken bones and wounds and allergic reactions.

BARBARA NIELSEN: We also deliver babies and sometimes have to subdue people who are violent and may harm others.

WALTER CARILLO: To be an Emergency Medical Technician, you have to be at least eighteen years old. In this state we take at least one hundred hours of training in basic emergency care.

JANICE: *(raises hand)* Do you work for a hospital?

BARBARA NIELSEN: Emergency Medical Technicians work for hospitals, for fire and police departments, for colleges, and for city and county governments. We are a two-person EMS ambulance team that works for a private EMS service. When you call 9-1-1 and request medical assistance, a dispatcher contacts the nearest available EMS team.

(SOUND: dispatch radio static. DISPATCHER speaks from offstage.)

DISPATCHER *(offstage)*: Truck 27, C-class run. Patient unresponsive, unknown if breathing.

BARBARA NIELSEN: This is a call to us from 9-1-1.

DISPATCHER *(offstage)*: Call-back in progress. Proceed to 404 Arundel Lane.

STEVE: Hey, that's my street! And 404 is Mrs. Bingham's house on the corner!

WALTER CARILLO: Let's go, people. It's an emergency!

(LIGHTS OUT BRIEFLY. SOUND: ambulance siren offstage. LIGHTS UP LEFT AND CENTER on MRS. BINGHAM sitting on box with MYRNA BRICE standing to her left comforting her with a Kleenex, a bag of groceries at her feet; Mrs. Bingham has her head bowed and her hands in her lap. Barbara Nielsen and Walter Carillo

approach her, followed by Mr. Brooks and the Class; Barbara Nielsen carries a medical supply bag over her shoulder; Barbara Nielsen and Walter Carillo each put on a pair of latex gloves.)

MYRNA BRICE: Oh, thank goodness, EMS is here! You'll be all right now, Mrs. Bingham, you'll be just fine.

(Barbara Nielsen sets down the medical bag and takes out a blood pressure cuff, while Walter Carillo takes a penlight from his pocket; he leans over Mrs. Bingham and visually examines her for external signs of injury.)

MYRNA BRICE: I called in the emergency. My name is Myrna Brice. Is she going to be all right?
WALTER CARILLO: We'll know more after we check her vital signs. *(to Mrs. Bingham)* Ma'am, can you hear me?
MRS. BINGHAM: *(dazedly)* Hmmm?
WALTER CARILLO: I said, can you hear me, ma'am?
MRS. BINGHAM: *(lifts her head slightly)* Yesss…yesss….
WALTER CARILLO: Good, she is responsive. And she seems to be breathing normally.

(Barbara Nielsen places the back of her hand against Mrs. Bingham's cheek.)

BARBARA NIELSEN: Her skin temperature is normal.

(Walter Carillo shines the penlight in Mrs. Bingham's eyes.)

WALTER CARILLO: Pupils are reactive.

(Barbara Nielsen places her thumb and forefinger against Mrs. Bingham's neck.)

BARBARA NIELSEN: I'm checking her carotid pulse. Pulse rate is a little high but not extreme.

(Barbara Nielsen takes her hand away from Mrs. Bingham's neck and lightly touches Mrs. Bingham's legs and shoulders.)

MYRNA BRICE: I was just coming back from the supermarket — those are my groceries right there, they were having a sale on pineapple yogurt mints — when I saw Mrs. Bingham here in her driveway. She was dragging that enormous trash can, and I waved and said hello, and she looked up and then, all of a sudden, she was down on the ground!

BARBARA NIELSEN: I don't feel any broken bones. Do you see any bleeding?

WALTER CARILLO: Doesn't appear to be. Ma'am, can you tell me if anything hurts?

MRS. BINGHAM: My wrist...*(tries to lift her right wrist)* Owwww!

WALTER CARILLO: She might have fallen on her wrist.

BARBARA NIELSEN: I'll get the icepack.

(Barbara Nielsen gets the icepack from the bag and hands it to Walter Carillo who gently holds Mrs. Bingham's wrist.)

MRS. BINGHAM: Mmmm...

WALTER CARILLO: This icepack will reduce the swelling.

(Barbara Nielsen applies blood pressure cuff to Mrs. Bingham's left arm.)

BARBARA NIELSEN: I'm going to check your blood pressure, Mrs. Bingham.
WALTER CARILLO: We'll keep this icepack here for a minute or so. Just rest easy.
MYRNA BRICE: It's just awful the things that happen to people when they get older. Can't even take out the trash without nearly losing your life!

(Walter Carillo looks to left of Mrs. Bingham and points to pill bottle on ground.)

WALTER CARILLO: What is that on the ground?

(Steve retrieves bottle and hands it to Walter Carillo, who studies it.)

STEVE: It looks like a pill bottle. Maybe Mrs. Bingham dropped it.
WALTER CARILLO: Have you been taking this medicine, ma'am?
MRS. BINGHAM: Hmmwhat?
WALTER CARILLO: I said, have you been taking this medicine?
MRS. BINGHAM: Yesss…for my neuralgia.
BARBARA NIELSEN: It might have side effects, such as dizziness, that affect her balance. We ought to take her in for X-rays and a more complete medical history.
MRS. BINGHAM: *(bows her head)* I feel…weak…
BARBARA NIELSEN: Mrs. Bingham, we think you just sprained your wrist, and you're going to be okay. But we'd like to take you to the emergency room to have a doctor check you over and give you a wrist support.

MRS. BINGHAM: Mmmm...all right...
WALTER CARILLO: Can you stand up, ma'am?
BARBARA NIELSEN: Easy does it. Here we go.
WALTER CARILLO: Good.

(Barbara Nielsen and Walter Carillo help Mrs. Bingham to her feet; A POLICEWOMAN enters from left.)

MYRNA BRICE: Oh my, here come the police!
POLICEWOMAN: Officer Rowley. How's everything going here?
BARBARA NIELSEN: Just fine, officer. Looks like a wrist injury. Thanks for stopping by.
POLICEWOMAN: Anytime I can, I do. A police officer often accompanies an EMS run to provide a safe working environment for the technicians. Let me give you a hand to the ambulance.

(Policewoman helps Walter Carillo walk Mrs. Bingham offstage left; Barbara Nielsen collects equipment and medical bag.)

BARBARA NIELSEN: Fortunately, this lady's injury doesn't appear to be life-threatening. But every time an EMS team arrives on the scene, we have to be ready for anything.
MR. BROOKS: The class certainly learned a lot today, Ms. Nielsen.
BARBARA NIELSEN: We're glad you were able to watch us work. So long! *(exits left)*
MR. BROOKS: And we're glad *you* were passing by, Ms. Brice.
MYRNA BRICE: Oh, it was nothing at all, nothing at all. I pass by here most days. Especially on Tuesday. That's trash day, don't you know.

STEVE: Gosh, maybe I'll start coming over before school on Tuesday and help Mrs. Bingham take her trash to the curb.

PAULA: You know, her garage looks kind of messy. I could come over after school one day and help her straighten out some of the boxes.

BURTON: I bet she has some neat old junk stuff packed away! I'll come, too!

JANICE: We could make it a class project and work together! And maybe Mr. Brooks would give us extra credit!

MR. BROOKS: That's an interesting idea, Janice. But we'd better wait until Mrs. Bingham gets home from the hospital — and *then* ask her how we can best help. Let's head back to school, shall we?

(Mr. Brooks leads Janice, Paula, Burton, and Steve offstage right, as Myrna Brice bends down to pick up her groceries.)

MYRNA BRICE: It's so nice to see young people acting thoughtful and kind.

(She struggles with the bag, groans, then turns toward stage right for help.)

MYRNA BRICE: Say there! Excuse me! Boys and girls, could I have your attention? *(shouts)* First one to pick up the bag gets a fresh pineapple yogurt mint! *(snorts, stamps her feet)* Hooligans! I guess I'm just going to have to call 9-1-1 to get any service here!

(LIGHTS OUT.)

THE END

Robots Are Everywhere
(Robotics Engineer)

Robots are used in almost every type of manufacturing and mining work you can imagine, as well as in the military and in outer space. In fact, the U.S. Bureau of Labor Statistics has forecast that by the year 2005 nearly one million jobs will be available in designing, making, and operating robots. Anyone working in the field of robotics must have extensive knowledge of computers, since most robots are controlled by computer microprocessors. In addition, most robotics jobs require college engineering courses that lead to at least a bachelor's degree. And, because of the impact working robots have on the jobs of humans, a robotics engineer must also have skills in psychology and economics.

If you want to get a head start in the field of robotics, why not try making your own? Check out these websites and library books:

http://www.xs4all.nl/~sbolt/e-index.html (Pitronics)
http://www.robotstore.com/index.html (Mondo-tronics Robot Store web site featuring almost 300 robot kits, books, and software)
Robots, androids, and animatrons: Twelve incredible projects you can build by John Iovine. Library call #: 629.892
The robot builder's bonanza: Ninety-nine inexpensive robotics projects by Gordon McComb. Library call #: 629.892

For information about a career as a robotics engineer, contact these sources:

Robotics International of SME, P.O. Box 930, One SME Drive, Dearborn, MI 48121. 313/271-1500.
http://www.frc.ri.cmu.edu/robotics-faq/ (Frequently Asked Questions List about Robotics)
http://www.robotmag.com/index.html (Robot Science and Technology Online)

RUNNING TIME: 15 minutes

CAST: 11 actors, minimum 4 boys (•), 4 girls (+)

+	Paula	•	Doug Martin, Robotics Lab Director
•	Burton	+	Polly, Robotics Engineer
+	Janice	•	Karl, Robotics Engineer
•	Steve		Sentry Robot
+	Ms. Vera, Teacher		Line Inspector Robot
			Fetch, a Retrieval Robot

STAGE SET: scrim or curtain at front of stage; behind are a table and a stool at mid center; a Sentry Robot stands to right of table; a Line Inspector Robot stands to left of table; further down and to the left of Line Inspector Robot stands Fetch

PROPS: clipboard, pencil, computer monitor and keyboard, miscellaneous robot parts

MUSIC: "Robots Everywhere"

COSTUMES: Paula, Burton, Janice, and Steve wear standard grade-school attire (Spring season); Burton wears a baseball cap and Janice has a bookbag on her back; Ms. Vera wears a standard female teacher's school outfit; Doug Martin, Polly, and Karl wear casual office clothes; robot characters can be covered in metallic-looking cloth or tinfoil with strings of tiny white or colored lights attached and topped by a face mask or boxy headgear — take a look at pictures of actual modern working robots to get more details

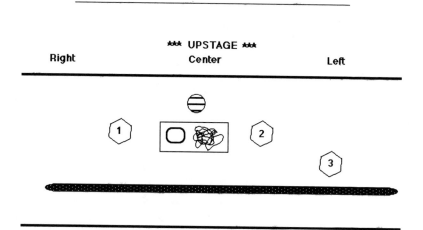

Stage Plan — *Robots Are Everywhere*

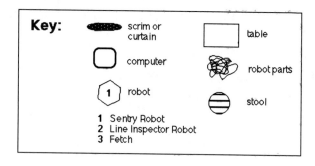

(LIGHTS UP FULL on BURTON and STEVE standing at down center. They stand stiffly with arms at sides, staring straight ahead at audience. They sing and march in place. Music: "Robots Everywhere.")

BURTON & STEVE: *(sing)*
Robots, robots, robots everywhere;
Trimming the lawn, milking the cows,
Cutting and perming your hair.

(JANICE and PAULA enter from left and march to down center, moving their arms and legs as if they were robots.)

BURTON & STEVE: *(sing)*
Cooking your meals, drilling for oil,
Washing the car, shoveling the snow,
Letting you know that robots will
Rule the world someday! Hey!

(Janice, Paula, Burton, and Steve link arms and march in place singing.)

ALL: *(sing)*
Robots, robots, robots, robots will
Rule the world someday! Hey!

(LIGHTS OUT. LIGHTS UP FULL after scrim or curtain rises revealing the robotics lab set. DOUG MARTIN stands at mid center writing on a clipboard, POLLY is seated at stool typing at the computer and KARL is adjusting the Line Inspector Robot at mid left. MS. VERA has entered from right and stands with Burton, Paula, Janice, and Steve at down center.)

MS. VERA: Today we're going to learn about the occupation of robotics engineer. Does anyone know what artificial intelligence is?

BURTON: *(raises hand)* Is it how smart you get after you eat a whole bunch of candy bars?

(Paula and Steve laugh; Janice raises her hand.)

MS. VERA: Yes, Janice?

JANICE: Artificial intelligence is when machines are programmed to perform activities that normally require human intelligence.

MS. VERA: Very good, Janice.

JANICE: Artificial intelligence is called "AI" for short.

MS. VERA: That's good, Janice.

JANICE: The mechanical devices that use AI are called "robots."

STEVE: *(aside loudly to Burton)* Janice *is* a robot!

(Paula, Burton, and Steve laugh; Janice raises her hand.)

MS. VERA: That's fine for now, Janice. Let's go into the lab.

(Ms. Vera and the students turn toward mid center, where Doug Martin greets them.)

DOUG MARTIN: Hi, there. I'm Doug Martin, director of Millennium Robotics, Incorporated. We are a company that makes designs for new robots. Did you know that there are more than two hundred thousand robots in the world today?

BURTON: Wow!

JANICE: Really?

STEVE: No way!

PAULA: Slammin'!

DOUG MARTIN: Robots are everywhere. They fish under the sea, they dig coal below the surface of the earth, they roam across planets in outer space. They even do brain surgery in hospitals.

BURTON: Coo-ool!

JANICE: Amazing!

STEVE: Yuck!

PAULA: Not on *my* brain!

DOUG MARTIN: Of course, robots are not new. In 1515 the great scientific genius of the Renaissance, Leonardo da Vinci, built a mechanical lion for the King of France. The famous American inventor Thomas Edison invented a talking doll in 1890. But it wasn't until 1962 that robots were first used to work in factories, which is where most robots are employed today.

STEVE: Is my model airplane a robot? It flies around by itself.

DOUG MARTIN: I'll let our engineers answer that. Meet Polly and Karl.

POLLY: If its actions come from its own computer program, then it's a real robot. If what it does comes from something you control, like a transmitter or joystick, it's just a toy.

KARL: All modern robots are controlled by microprocessors. The microprocessors are controlled by computer programs that robotics engineers like Polly and I develop.

POLLY: If you want to be a robotics engineer, you have to know a lot about computers.

KARL: You need at least a bachelor's degree in engineering.

POLLY: I have a master's degree in industrial engineering. And you'll take training in hydraulics and pneumatics, integrated systems and logic and computer-aided design and manufacturing.

KARL: Many people working in the robotics field also have degrees in psychology, sociology, business, and art design.

POLLY: With robotics, your learning never stops. We always have to stay up-to-date on new developments in the field.

DOUG MARTIN: Most importantly, you have to work well as a team member. There are many phases to designing a robot. Not every engineer can do the whole job alone.

KARL: Polly and I are the test-phase engineers. Before the robot gets to us, it's been with other engineers who plan the computer program—

POLLY: And develop cost proposals—

KARL: And efficiency studies—

POLLY: And quality control reports.

DOUG MARTIN: But working with robots is a lot of fun. Take a look at this project Polly's working on. It's a Sentry Robot, designed to patrol an office or warehouse just like a human security guard.

(Class gathers around the SENTRY ROBOT at mid right.)

POLLY: The Sentry Robot uses microwaves to sense movement and detect sound. This is a second generation model we're programming to sense dangerous smells, such as smoke or leaking gas.

STEVE: *(aside loudly to Paula)* Or Burton's underwear!

(Polly flicks a switch on the Sentry Robot's back, and the robot starts to move slowly forward, one small step at a time; children recoil a bit.)

BURTON: Yo!
JANICE: Yipe!
STEVE: Mon dieu!
PAULA: Bust-out!

(Sentry Robot halts at edge of stage.)

SENTRY ROBOT: *(monotonally)* No ex-tran-e-ous o-dors de-tec-ted. I will re-turn to base.

(Sentry Robot moves slowly backward, one small step at a time, to original position where Polly flicks its back switch to Off.)

POLLY: Right now this robot can travel only a few feet. When we're finished, it will be able to patrol an entire city block.
KARL: Over here is a Line Inspector Robot.

(Class gathers around the LINE INSPECTOR ROBOT at mid left.)

KARL: Robot, what general function do you perform?
LINE INSPECTOR ROBOT: *(monotonally)* Gen-e-ral func-tion: to de-tect and re-port...break-age of in-su-la-tor caps...in e-lec-tri-cal pow-er...ca-bles.
JANICE: It understood what you said!
KARL: Usually this robot sends its data straight to another computer. But while it's in the lab I've programmed it to respond to my voice.
PAULA: Could you ask it something else? Like, what color the sky is? Or what is the capital of North Dakota?
KARL: That information isn't programmed in its software because it isn't vital to its main function. However, if you

ask something about power cables, this robot can process an answer at a speed of twenty M.I.P.S. — that's *millions* of instructions per second.

(Ms. Vera turns to FETCH standing at down left.)

MS. VERA: And who is this curious-looking creature?

(Paula, Janice, Steve, and Burton gather around Fetch, staring at it closely, pointing and whispering among themselves.)

POLLY: That's a retrieval robot called Fetch. Karl and I designed Fetch to pick up litter around the lab.
KARL: Fetch is a very efficient retriever. When Fetch is on the trail of something, he's like a bloodhound.
BURTON: Woof-woof!
PAULA: *(nudges Burton)* Burton!
JANICE: Why isn't Fetch retrieving now?
KARL: There's been a slight software problem. Fetch is being repaired.
DOUG MARTIN: Good work, engineers. Any questions from our visitors?

(Everyone turns away from Fetch and faces right toward Doug Martin at down center; Burton remains standing next to Fetch.)

STEVE: *(raises hand)* Can a robot ever do bad things?
DOUG MARTIN: A robot might injure a person or destroy property by accident. But a robot doesn't think beyond its programming. For example, it doesn't have the motivation to work harder to get a promotion. Or have the

desire to take something not needed to do its job. And it certainly could never, *ever* harbor any sort of hostility.

(Fetch knocks Burton's hat off; Burton whirls around but Fetch has returned to its immobile position; throughout the next few lines Burton continues to glance back at Fetch, which remains immobile.)

PAULA: Oh, not that it would *mean* to...but if its programming went bad?

POLLY: Anything is possible if there's a programming error.

KARL: Our programs have self-correcting mechanisms. The robot would shut down until the problem was fixed. Like Fetch here.

DOUG MARTIN: Does that make everyone feel better? Remember, robots are meant to be our friends.

(Fetch knocks Burton's hat off; Burton whirls around but Fetch has returned to its immobile position.)

BURTON: Ms. Vera!

MS. VERA: That's all we have time for today, class. Thank you, engineers. We've all learned a lot about a fascinating field of science.

BURTON: I'll say!

MS. VERA: Burton, please!

(Ms. Vera turns and exits right followed by Paula, Janice, Steve, and — bringing up the rear — Burton, who keeps turning to look suspiciously at Fetch, which remains immobile. As Burton is about to exit, he turns and pauses, not quite looking back at Fetch but thinking about it.)

FETCH: Pllllppp! *(wiggles hands in ears and emits raspberry sound)*

(Burton looks at Fetch and sees it mocking him, then turns and exits yelling.)

BURTON: Ms. Ver-aaaaaaa!

(LIGHTS OUT.)

THE END

Heave Away, Haul Away!
(Tugboat Captain)

Though we are long past the days of clipper ships and paddle-wheeled riverboats, the sea is very much part of our national economy — one of every six American jobs is related to the sea and its commerce. Serving as a ship's captain is a position of great responsibility, whether the vessel be a sleek ocean liner or squat harbor tugboat; the captain is on call every minute the ship is on the water and must be ready to attend to any emergency that arises. Tugboats and their crews are generally hired for short periods of time, usually to perform a particular task such as pushing a barge from one end of the harbor to the other. Tugboats with ice-breaking equipment attached to their prows are hired during winter to clear rivers and port entrances for bigger boats. Most tugboat captains have served on some sort of seagoing vessel from an early age; many are skilled boat builders, navigators, and engineers. Increasingly, even tugboats sail with the aid of computers and electronic directional systems, so a tugboat captain must also have experience in these areas as well.

For information about a career as a tugboat operator or building tugboats, contact these sources:

American Institute of Merchant Shipping, 1000 Sixteenth Street NW, #511, Washington, DC 20023-5705. 202/775-4399.
http://www.tugboats.com/ (Tugboat Crossing)

http://www.halcyon.com/aslocke/welcome.htm (The Mini-Tugboat Home Page)

International Tug & Salvage and *Tug World Magazine*: 19 Bridge Road, East Molesey, Surrey, ENGLAND, KT8 9EU. *E-mail:* tugsrus@abreed.demon.co.uk

---

RUNNING TIME: 20 minutes

CAST: 25 actors, minimum 4 boys (•), 3 girls (+)

+	Paula	•	Captain Gray, Tugboat Captain
•	Burton		First Mate
+	Janice		Engineer
•	Steve,		Pilot
+	Ms. Vera, Teacher		Deckhand
	2 Colonial Era Indians	•	Captain Burke, Pirate
	2 18th-century Voyageurs		2 Pirate Henchmen
	3 19th-century Pioneers		2 Gold Rush 49ers
	3 World War I Soldiers		

STAGE SET: at down right a ramp that rises to the boat's main deck at mid right — a platform approximately twelve feet wide, eight feet deep and one foot high that extends to mid center where there is either another platform (four feet wide, four feet deep, one foot high) or simply an enclosed booth with windows on all sides that represents the boat's wheelhouse; to the left of the wheelhouse (on the main deck platform) are two three-foot high posts ("forward bitts"); a rail extends along the main deck except for the boat's bow; at down left is a large stone or boulder; there should be two entrances on the left side of the stage, one at down left, the other at mid or up left *

PROPS: thick rope (six-feet length), oil rag, lug wrench, binoculars, five life jackets for Ms. Vera and Class, spade, eighteenth-century pistol, cutlass, treasure chest, two canoe paddles, fur hat, animal pelt, pickax, three World War I rifles

MUSIC: "Bound for South Australia," "The Flying Cloud," "Ojibway Canoe Song," "Dans Les Chantiers Nous Hivernerons," "Shenadoah," "Sacramento," "When Johnny Comes Marching Home"

EFFECTS: Sound — klunk of tow pushing into barge

COSTUMES: Paula, Burton, Janice, and Steve wear standard grade-school attire (Spring season); Burton wears a baseball cap and Janice has a bookbag on her back; Ms. Vera wears a standard female teacher's school outfit; Captain Gray and the tugboat crew wear T-shirts, blue jeans, and workboots; Captain Burke and Pirate Henchmen dress as eighteenth-century Caribbean pirates, Captain Burke with a black eye-patch; Colonial Era Indians wear Woodland Indian garb — a fringed buckskin vest, feathered headdress, brown moccasins; eighteenth-century Voyageurs wear light linen shirt and buckskin breeches held up by a wide leather belt, a large low-brimmed beaver hat and moccasins; nineteenth-century Pioneers and Gold Rush 49ers wear plain shirts, jeans, boots, Western hats and/or bonnets for the women; World War I Soldiers wear standard khaki doughboy uniform and helmet

* <u>Nautical</u> <u>Terms</u>: The *bow* of a boat is the front; the *stern* is the rear; *port* side is the side of the boat to the left; *starboard* side is to the right.

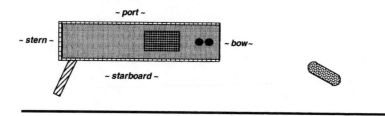

Stage Plan — *Heave Away, Haul Away!*

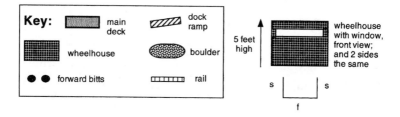

(LIGHTS UP FULL on JANICE, PAULA, BURTON, and STEVE standing at down center facing audience. They sing "Bound for South Australia.")

PAULA: *(sings)* In South Australia I was born!
BURTON, JANICE, & STEVE: *(sing)* Heave away, haul away!
PAULA: *(sings)* Ten thousand miles beyond Cape Horn!
BURTON, JANICE, & STEVE: *(sing)* We're bound for South Australia!
ALL: *(sing)*
    Heave away, you rolling kings!
    Heave away, haul away!
    Heave away and hear me sing!
    We're bound for South Australia!

(MS. VERA enters from left, clapping her hands.)

MS. VERA: That's a wonderful shanty song, class. But we don't have to go as far as Australia to learn about people who make their living by working on the water. We're going to visit a tugboat right on our own river.

(CAPTAIN GRAY enters from right and strides forward to down center to greet the Class.)

MS. VERA: And here's the Captain.

CAPTAIN GRAY: Welcome aboard *The Mudcat* — a little boat that does a lot of big work! I'm Captain Gray, and this morning we'll be pushing a sand barge to the other side of the harbor. Let's climb on the main deck, shall we? Mind the plank!

(Ms. Vera leads the Class up the dock ramp to the main deck at mid right. Captain Gray stands.)

CAPTAIN GRAY: The job of a tugboat is to move bigger boats and barges through inland waterways. They travel along rivers and bays and canals. Did you know that twelve thousand ships a year dock in this very harbor? The big ships depend on the little tugboats to guide them safely in to shore and out to sea again.

JANICE: *(raises hand)* I don't see any sails, Captain Gray? How does the tugboat move on the water?

CAPTAIN GRAY: By horsepower, young lady! In this case, a seven-hundred-fifty-horsepower diesel engine.

STEVE: *(raises hand)* That sounds like a big engine. How fast does a tugboat go?

CAPTAIN GRAY: *The Mudcat* can travel at a speed of ten

nautical miles an hour. On land, you don't walk any quicker than three miles yourself.

(FIRST MATE enters main deck from behind wheelhouse and greets the Class with a friendly wave.)

CAPTAIN GRAY: Ah, here's our first mate!
FIRST MATE: This is a fine-looking crew! I hope every one of you lads and lasses is ready to rig the hawser and hoist the winch!
BURTON, PAULA, STEVE, & JANICE: Yay!
FIRST MATE: Just pulling your sea legs, skippers. That sort of work is reserved for me and my deckhands.

(DECKHAND enters main deck from behind wheelhouse and goes to the forward bitts; he carries a thick rope; Class moves closer and stands next to the wheelhouse.)

FIRST MATE: There's my top man now. Ahoy, sailor!
DECKHAND: I've got to tie this cable around these posts — called bitts — and then tie them to the bitts on the barge we're going to push. Once you're out in the water, you don't want your load floating away. *(wraps rope around forward bitts)*

(ENGINEER enters main deck from behind wheelhouse and stands next to the Deckhand; Engineer wipes his wrench with an oil rag.)

ENGINEER: Hello, I'm *The Mudcat's* engineer. I work below deck, taking care of the engine, checking oil levels and temperatures, minding the pressure gauges. *(displays wrench and rag)* As you can see, I spend a lot of time cleaning up broken and wornout parts.

(PILOT peers out from wheelhouse window, binoculars around his neck.)

PILOT: And I'm the pilot. I'm the crazy fool who drives this old tank. In the old days all I had was a steering wheel and maybe enough sense to know which way the wind was blowing. Now, I've got depth finders, magnetic compasses, weather radio and radar that shows me every ship for miles around. Tugboats do a lot of travelling in night and fog, you know.

CAPTAIN GRAY: Lucky for us, it's bright and clear this morning! First mate, pass out the life jackets!

(First Mate gives life jackets to Ms. Vera and Class, who put them on; Engineer crosses to bow and stands next to Deckhand at forward bitts.)

FIRST MATE: Stand steady!
MS. VERA: Class, take hold of the rail!

(Ms. Vera and Class take hold of the rail at stern and port side; Captain Gray and First Mate stand at front rail and look to mid left.)

CAPTAIN GRAY: Cast off!
FIRST MATE: Cast off!
DECKHAND: Casting off!

(Deckhand pulls rope tight around forward bitts as tugboat begins pushing barge forward; SOUND: offstage klunk of tow pushing into barge; all characters roll slightly to left, then back again to upright position.)

PILOT: We're away!

FIRST MATE: We're away!

(During the ensuing voyage, Deckhand and Engineer look to mid left and occasionally adjust rope around forward bitts; Pilot looks to mid left also, maintaining vigil with binoculars.)

FIRST MATE: You can loosen your hold on the side rails, folks. But don't wander too far away. The water in this bay can be a bit choppy.

MS. VERA: *(to Captain Gray)* How long is our trip, Captain?

CAPTAIN GRAY: We'll dock in an hour, ma'am. If the weather holds fair, it'll be an easy voyage.

BURTON: *(to Steve)* Yeh, a *slow* voyage! They should call this boat *The Snail!*

STEVE: *(to Burton)* Really! This is the dullest field trip we've had yet.

PAULA: *(raises hand)* Captain, sir? Do you sail this same way every day?

CAPTAIN GRAY: You bet! Sometimes three or four times.

JANICE: *(raises hand)* Does it ever get kind of boring after awhile? I mean you just see the same scenery every day!

CAPTAIN GRAY: Boring? *(laughs heartily, then points toward audience)* Look on that shore yonder, and tell me what you see.

(Ms. Vera and the Class look toward audience as CAPTAIN BURKE enters from down left, followed by TWO PIRATE HENCHMEN, one of whom carries a spade, the other a treasure chest. PIRATE #1 sets chest down behind boulder and sits on boulder, fingering the pistol in his belt while PIRATE #2 begins digging a hole in front of boulder; Captain Burke watches the digging with his cutlass drawn.)

BURTON: *(shrugs)* I dunno. A bunch of trees. And some old warehouses.

CAPTAIN GRAY: I'll tell you what I see. I see history. The history of this great country — coming alive with every whisper of the wind! *(points down left)* Look sharp! There's Captain Burke and his pirates!

(Ms. Vera and the Class look down left; Captain Burke strides forward to down center, slashing the air with his cutlass.)

CAPTAIN GRAY: Captain Burke was commander of *The Scarab,* the bloodiest buccaneer from Point Royal to Cape Bedford. Late one night in 1681, Burke and two of his fiercest henchmen came ashore to bury a load of treasure.

CAPTAIN BURKE: Make haste, lads! The tide's heading out!

(MUSIC: Two Pirate Henchmen sing "The Flying Cloud.")

TWO PIRATE HENCHMEN: *(sing)*
Come all you loyal seamen, wherever you may be,
I am here bound down in irons to die in piracy;
With eighty or more of my brave men, in sorrow and in pain,
All for robbing and a-pillaging down on the Spanish Main.

(Captain Burke strides to boulder.)

CAPTAIN BURKE: Aye, that's a grand job of digging, maties! *(to Pirate #1)* Give him his due!

(Pirate #1 shoots Pirate #2, who falls dead.)

CAPTAIN BURKE: Aye, now here's *your* reward! *(stabs Pirate #1 with cutlass; Pirate #2 falls dead)*

(Captain Burke brandishes cutlass and laughs wickedly.)

CAPTAIN BURKE: Dead men tell no tales! *(exits up left; Two Pirate Henchmen drag off up left)*
CAPTAIN GRAY: Burke returned to his ship but was sunk the next day in battle. They say on a moonlit night, his ghost comes back to shore looking for the treasure.
BURTON: Co-ool!

(TWO INDIANS enter from down left, each holding a canoe paddle and facing audience.)

CAPTAIN GRAY: And well before that, there were Native American tribes who fished the bountiful rivers nearby.

(MUSIC: Two Indians sing "Ojibway Canoe Song.")

TWO INDIANS: *(sing)*
Che-kah-bay / te-bick / on-dan-dey-an
Che-kah-bay / te-bick / on-dan-dey-an
Ah-gah-mah-si-bi / on-dan-dey-an

(Two Indians exit up left, as TWO VOYAGEURS enter from down left, each holding a fur hat or animal pelt and facing audience.)

CAPTAIN GRAY: Later on, fur trappers came from Canada and built a trading post right where that fuel depot is now.

(MUSIC: Two Voyageurs sing "Dans Les Chantiers Nous Hivernerons.")

TWO VOYAGEURS: *(sing)*
    Voici l'hiver arrivé, les rivieres sont gelées.
    C'est le temps d'aller au bois, manger du lard et des pois.
    Dans les chantiers nous hivernerons!
    Dans les chantiers nous hivernerons!

    Lo, the winter now has come, and the river frozen over.
    It is time to go to hunt, eating pork and beans galore.
    To camp we'll go till the winter's gone!
    To camp we'll go till the winter's gone!

(Two Voyageurs exit up left, as THREE PIONEERS enter from down left and face audience.)

CAPTAIN GRAY: *(points down left)* Look! There goes a young pioneer family catching the flatboat to their homestead in the West!

(MUSIC: Three Pioneers sing "Shenandoah.")

THREE PIONEERS: *(sing)*
    O, Shenandoah, I long to hear you;
    Away you rolling river!
    O, Shenandoah, I long to hear you;
    Away, I'm bound away,
    Across the wide Missouri!

(Three Pioneers exit up left, as TWO 49ERS carrying spade and pickax enter from down left and face audience.)

JANICE: *(raises hand)* Didn't a lot of people leave here for the California Gold Rush?

CAPTAIN GRAY: They certainly did. The old steamboat dock was right by that highway bridge.

(MUSIC: Two 49ers sing "Sacramento.")

TWO 49ERS: *(sing)*
>A bully ship and a bully crew!
>Hoo-dah! Hoo-dah!
>A bully mate and a skipper, too!
>All the hoo-dah day!
>
>Then blow you winds, hi-ho!
>For Californi-o!
>There's plenty of gold so I've been told
>In Sacramenti-o!

(Two 49ers exit up left, as THREE SOLDIERS carrying rifles enter from down left and face audience standing in drill formation.)

PAULA: *(raises hand, points down left)* And that yacht club? What did that used to be?

CAPTAIN GRAY: During the first World War, it was a recruiting station for the army. It was the last sight of home many young soldiers ever saw.

(MUSIC: Three Soldiers sing "When Johnny Comes Marching Home Again.")

THREE SOLDIERS: *(sing)*
>When Johnny comes marching home again,
>Hurrah! Hurrah!

We'll give him a hearty welcome then,
Hurrah! Hurrah!
The men will cheer, the boys will shout,
The ladies they will all turn out,
And we'll all feel proud when Johnny comes marching home!

(Three Soldiers exit down left marching.)

BURTON: Gosh, Ms. Vera, the Captain's right — there sure *is* a lot of neat history around here!
STEVE: Indians and pirates and soldiers! This is the best field trip we've ever had!
PILOT: We're almost to dock!

(All characters look to mid left as tug pushes barge into dock; crew becomes very intense.)

CAPTAIN GRAY: Go over to channel seven!
PILOT: Roger, switching to seven!
ENGINEER: Mind the buoy to starboard!
CAPTAIN GRAY: Back a bit to port!
PILOT: Backing to port!
CAPTAIN GRAY: Back a hair straight rudder!
PILOT: Backing straight rudder!
CAPTAIN GRAY: Where's the turning mark, pilot?
DECKHAND: Five degrees left rudder!
CAPTAIN GRAY: Five degrees left!
PILOT: Five degrees left!
FIRST MATE: There's your mark!
CAPTAIN GRAY: Cut her forty-five degrees to starboard!
PILOT: Forty-five starboard!
CAPTAIN GRAY: Hold on station! Set for approach!
PILOT: Set!

FIRST MATE: Back her down!
CAPTAIN GRAY: Easy on the throttle! Back her down!
PILOT: Pointing for the middle!
DECKHAND: Threading the needle!
ENGINEER: Coming home!
CAPTAIN GRAY: Hold steady!
PILOT: Holding!
FIRST MATE: Stand steady!
MS. VERA: Class, take hold of the rail!

(Ms. Vera and Class take hold of the rail at stern and port side. SOUND: offstage klunk of barge pushing into dock; all characters roll slightly to right, then back again to upright position.)

PILOT: We're home!
FIRST MATE: Home!
CAPTAIN GRAY, ENGINEER, & DECKHAND: Home!
BURTON, PAULA, STEVE, & JANICE: Hurrah!

(Deckhand and Engineer loosen rope from forward bitts as Ms. Vera and Class move toward dock ramp.)

MS. VERA: Thank you for taking us on the trip.
CAPTAIN GRAY: Glad you could watch us work. The mighty *Mudcat* is always at your service.
FIRST MATE: Careful down the plank!

(Ms. Vera leads Janice, Paula, Steve, and Burton down the ramp; all exit right except for Burton, who stops to tie his shoelace.)

MS. VERA: *(offstage right)* Line up single file for the bus!
BURTON: Hey, Steve, wait up!

STEVE: *(offstage right)* Come on, Burton!

BURTON: Hold your horses! Hey, how about those wild stories? *(still looking at his feet)* You know what? I think that captain made 'em all up!

(As Burton finishes tying and rises, Captain Burke enters from down left and stands at the boulder with cutlass drawn, looking toward audience.)

CAPTAIN BURKE: Aye, that's a grand job of tying, matey!

(Burton looks to his left; freezes briefly, then runs screaming offstage right.)

BURTON: *(offstage right)* Whaaaaa!

(LIGHTS OUT.)

THE END

The Flying Cloud
(traditional, arr. by L.E. McCullough)

Ojibway Canoe Song
(traditional, arr. by L.E. McCullough)

Dans Les Chantiers Nous Hivernerons
**(traditional, arr. by L.E. McCullough;
English words by Frederic Burget)**

Sacramento

(music: Stephen Foster, words: traditional, arr. by L.E. McCullough)

Shenandoah

(traditional, arr. by L.E. McCullough)

When Johnny Comes Marching Home Again
(words & music: Patrick S. Gilmore, arr. by L.E. McCullough)

The Case of the Purple Pen
(Crime Lab Technician)

Crime lab technicians employ science and technology in helping police solve crimes. After police collect evidence at a crime scene, the technician analyzes it for clues to aid the investigation. Often, the crime lab technician prepares the evidence for presentation in court. Though they are not police officers themselves, most crime lab technicians work closely with some sort of law enforcement agency, ranging from local and state police to the FBI. Crime laboratories typically require a college degree in crime technology, a course of study that includes classes in laboratory and police methods. Crime lab technicians must have a strong scientific research background to keep up with the many ongoing advances in crime-solving technology. They must also have a great deal of patience and precision, since much of their work can result in determining guilt and innocence of suspected criminals.

For information about a career as a crime lab technician, contact these sources:

International Association of Chiefs of Police, 515 N. Washington Street, Alexandria, VA 22314. 703/836-6767.
http://www.uwm.edu/Dept/CJ/ (Criminal Justice Programs at University of Wisconsin-Milwaukee)
http://zeno.simplenet.com/general.htm (Zeno's Forensic Page)
http://www.geocities.com/CapeCanaveral/6635/ (Forensic Science Education Resource)

RUNNING TIME: 15 minutes

CAST: 12 actors, minimum 3 boys (•), 4 girls (+)
- \+ Paula
- • Burton
- \+ Janice
- • Steve
- \+ Ms. Vera, Teacher
- \+ Donna, Burton's Older Sister
- • Mr. Hanafin, Crime Lab Supervisor
-   Ballistics Technician
-   Documents Technician
-   Instruments Technician
-   Polygraph Technician
-   Chemical/Physical Analysis Technician

STAGE SET: scrim or curtain at front of stage; behind are two long tables, one small table, five stools

PROPS: book, invisible dog leash, bubble gum, purple pen, wristwatch, small plastic envelope, microscope, x-ray machine, spectrograph, polygraph, small twenty-inch bicycle

COSTUMES: Paula, Burton, Janice, and Steve wear standard grade-school attire (Spring season); Burton wears a baseball cap and Janice has a bookbag on her back; Donna wears sixth-grade clothing style; Ms. Vera wears a standard female teacher's school outfit; Mr. Hanafin wears a suit and tie; Lab Technicians wear white lab coats over dress shirts/blouses and slacks

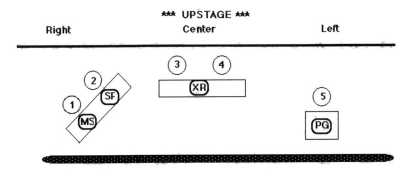

Stage Plan — *The Case of the Purple Pen*

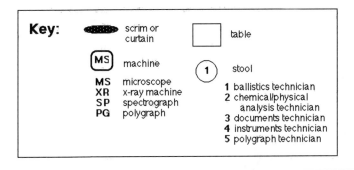

(LIGHTS UP FULL; SCRIM OR CURTAIN IS DOWN; PAULA enters from left and skips to down center, singing "Zip-A-Dee-Doo-Dah" in full voice.)

PAULA: *(sings)* Zip-a-dee-doo-dah! Zip-a-dee-hey! I don't wanna go to schoo-ool today! *(turns to audience and begins snapping fingers and rapping)*

Even though it's only Monday
My fingers can't help snappin;
I got a funny feeling
Something big is gonna happen!

(BURTON enters from right, frantic and peering around wildly.)

PAULA: Hi, Burton! What are you looking for?

BURTON: Paula! Did you see it? Tell me you saw it! Please tell me you saw it!

PAULA: See what?

BURTON: My bike! Somebody stole my bike!

PAULA: Stole it? Weren't you riding it when you left your house?

BURTON: Wellllll...I *was*...but I...well, I got off for a minute or two.

PAULA: Got off? Why?

BURTON: Wellllll...

PAULA: Let me guess...you stopped at the drugstore?

BURTON: Wellllll...

PAULA: And you bought some—

(Burton blows a big gum bubble.)

PAULA: Bubble gum!

BURTON: It was calling my name!

PAULA: Bubble gum doesn't talk, Burton.

BURTON: It does to me!

PAULA: When you came out the bike was gone.

BURTON: My mom and dad are gonna ground me forever! Paula what am I going to do?

PAULA: Have you thought about emigrating to Greenland? I hear the tundra is quite refreshing this time of year.

BURTON: Do they have bubble gum there?

(JANICE, a bookbag on her back, enters from left, reading a book as she walks to down center.)

PAULA: We'll ask Janice. She has a brain the size of South America.
JANICE: Hey, guys! How come you're just standing here? You'll be late for school.
BURTON: I don't think I'll make it to school today, Janice. I don't feel so good.
JANICE: What's wrong, Burton? You look sick to your stomach.
PAULA: And he hasn't even swallowed his gum yet.
BURTON: My bike got stolen. Right outside the drugstore.
JANICE: That's terrible! Who could do such a mean, rotten, craven thing?
PAULA: Someone from Rotten Craven Meanies, Incorporated?
BURTON: I found this next to where I parked the bike. *(holds up a pen)*
JANICE: It's a pen! The thief must have dropped it.
BURTON: It wasn't there when I went inside. *(gives pen to Janice, who peers at it closely)*
PAULA: *(points to pen)* A purple pen. Why does it have those red streaks on it?

(STEVE enters from right holding invisible dog leash and pretending to walk a dog; he jerkily crosses to down center.)

STEVE: Whoa, boy, whoa! Easy does it, Fantôme!
JANICE: Steve! School is the other way!
STEVE: Just following my dog, Fantôme.
BURTON: Huh? I don't see any dog.
JANICE: Fantôme — it's French for phantom or ghost. Invisible dog, get it?
STEVE: *(bows)* C'est bon, mademoiselle! C'est bon!
PAULA: Well, in plain English, somebody stole Burton's bike!
JANICE: And we found a clue! *(holds up pen)*
STEVE: Well, this is a special day for sure!

THE CASE OF THE PURPLE PEN 103

BURTON: Yeh, *too* special! My bike's gone, and I'm grounded through eternity!
STEVE: No, it really *is* special. We're going on a field trip today. Don't you remember?
PAULA: Field trip? Where?
STEVE: To the police station. To visit the crime lab.
BURTON, PAULA, & JANICE: Crime lab!
STEVE: We can have them help us find out who stole Burton's bike!
BURTON, PAULA, & JANICE: Let's go!

(Burton, Paula, and Janice exit right; Steve lags behind, pulling on his leash.)

STEVE: Come on, doggie! Nice doggie, come on! Rrrrrrr! Woof-woof!

(LIGHTS OUT as Steve exits. LIGHTS UP FULL after scrim or curtain rises revealing the crime lab set. BALLISTICS TECHNICIAN, CHEMICAL/PHYSICAL ANALYSIS TECHNICIAN, DOCUMENTS TECHNICIAN, and INSTRUMENTS TECHNICIAN are seated on stools at their places; MR. HANAFIN stands at up center talking to Instrument Technician. MS. VERA enters from right, leading Burton, Paula, Janice, and Steve and pausing at down right.)

MS. VERA: Now, class, we are about to visit a real crime lab. This is where evidence is examined that may be used in police investigations. Remember that this is a place of work, and everyone you see is very busy working. So please be quiet and polite and keep your hands to yourself at all times. Watch, listen...and learn.
BURTON: *(raises hand)* Ms. Vera!

MS. VERA: What is it, Burton?
BURTON: May we chew bubble gum in the crime lab?

(Ms. Vera does not reply but stares sternly at Burton as Paula and Steve giggle and Janice rolls her eyes.)

BURTON: *(lowers hand)* I'll take that as a "no."

(Mr. Hanafin steps forward and offers his hand to Ms. Vera, who shakes it.)

MR. HANAFIN: Hello, there! You must be the school tour group. Welcome to the police crime lab. My name is Mr. Hanafin, the lab supervisor.
MS. VERA: I am Ms. Vera, and we are very eager to learn about what a crime lab technician does.
MR. HANAFIN: First of all, there are many types of crime lab technicians, and each technician has his or her own special area of expertise. But everyone who works in a crime lab works toward the same goal — to analyze the physical evidence found at the scene of an accident or crime. If we do our job right, we are able to help police investigators solve the crime and identify the guilty party.
JANICE: Can't you also use evidence to prove an innocent person not guilty?
MR. HANAFIN: Yes, indeed, a crime lab technician often turns up evidence that helps clear a suspect who might have been unfairly charged with a crime. Now, let's say a crime has been committed, say—
STEVE: Somebody's bike has been stolen.
MR. HANAFIN: All right. That is called a "larceny," which is the taking of another person's property without their permission.
BURTON: I'll say!

MR. HANAFIN: First, let's visit our Ballistics Technician.

(Mr. Hanafin leads the class to Ballistics Technician, who is seated and examining evidence under a microscope.)

BALLISTICS TECHNICIAN: Ballistics is the science that examines the motion and force of projectiles — usually, bullets fired from a gun. Was any shooting involved in the larceny?

BURTON: I don't think so.

BALLISTICS TECHNICIAN: If there had been, and the bullets had been found, I would use this microscope to examine them. I would be able to discover what type of gun had fired the bullets and what company had manufactured them. That might tell us where they had been purchased — and by whom.

MR. HANAFIN: Was there *any* piece of evidence found at the crime scene?

PAULA: Just this pen! *(holds up the pen)*

MR. HANAFIN: Well, I guess we had better see our Chemical and Physical Analysis Technician.

(Mr. Hanafin leads the class to Chemical/Physical Analysis Technician, who is seated and examining evidence under a spectrograph.)

CHEMICAL/PHYSICAL ANALYSIS TECHNICIAN: Greetings! My specialty is studying fragments and residues — little tiny bits of anything found on items at the crime scene. This spectrograph here can enlarge the tiniest bits of evidence. Dirt, hair, blood, glass, paint, food crumbs, you name it.

(Paula lays pen in front of Chemical/Physical Analysis Technician, who looks at it without touching it.)

PAULA: Would you be able to find out about these red streaks on the purple pen?

CHEMICAL/PHYSICAL ANALYSIS TECHNICIAN: I'd be able to enlarge the streaks so their basic pattern could be seen and compared with other similar patterns. Then we could discover what that streak was made of and what might have put it there.

MR. HANAFIN: Did you find any scraps of paper on the ground?

BURTON: I didn't see any.

DOCUMENTS TECHNICIAN: If you had found some, I'd have a look. I'm the Documents Technician. I analyze handwriting and types of paper and ink. Besides this spectrograph, I also make use of infrared photography and ultraviolet light to reveal secrets hidden between the lines.

PAULA: Do you analyze kidnap notes?

DOCUMENTS TECHNICIAN: You bet.

STEVE: And death threats?

DOCUMENTS TECHNICIAN: Some of those, too, along with forged checks, blackmail letters, and everyday diaries.

INSTRUMENTS TECHNICIAN: Were there any instruments found at the scene?

BURTON: You mean, like a tuba?

INSTRUMENTS TECHNICIAN: No, son. The instruments I'm talking about are objects used in the crime — perhaps a hammer or stone that might have broken the bike lock. I'm an Instruments Technician, and my job is to match the marks found at the scene to the instruments, or objects, that made them.

JANICE: I guess we'd better look again after school.

PAULA: But what about fingerprints on this pen? Won't they tell us something?

MR. HANAFIN: They'll tell us about *your* fingerprints. How many of the rest of you have touched this pen?

(Sheepishly, Burton, Janice, and Steve raise their hands; Mr. Hanafin draws a small plastic envelope from his pocket.)

MR. HANAFIN: This is an "evidence envelope." Police officers and technicians carry them at all times. *(directs Paula to place pen in envelope, which she does)* By putting your evidence in the envelope and sealing it securely within, you prevent your evidence from being contaminated — in this case having what may have been the thief's fingerprints covered over by all of yours.

(Mr. Hanafin seals envelope and hands it back to Paula, who hands it to Janice, who hands it to Burton, who hands it to Steve, who shrugs and sticks it in his pocket.)

MS. VERA: Do Fingerprint Technicians only study fingerprints?

MR. HANAFIN: No, ma'am. They also analyze footprints, tire treads, bite marks, and other impressions left by criminals or their instruments. And, along with a Fingerprint Technician, we always send a Photographer to the crime scene to take photographs and develop them back here at the lab.

JANICE: I have a pretty good camera. Can I get a job working in the crime lab?

MR. HANAFIN: Not quite yet. All crime lab technicians must have a strong background in science. Taking lots of math, biology, chemistry, and physics is a good start. Once you get in college, you'll want to take courses in scientific crime detection and earn a degree in Crime Technology.

MS. VERA: I suppose a crime lab technician never stops learning.

MR. HANAFIN: That's right, ma'am. You always have to keep up-to-date on the newest techniques in the field.

STEVE: So you can keep one step ahead of the criminals!

MR. HANAFIN: And bring them to justice. Speaking of which, here comes our Polygraph Technician.

(POLYGRAPH TECHNICIAN enters from left and sits on stool, adjusting the polygraph; Mr. Hanafin, Ms. Vera, and the class approach.)

POLYGRAPH TECHNICIAN: My job is to use this machine — the polygraph — to give what's called a "lie detector test" to people we think may have information about a crime. They may be a suspect, or they may be a witness.

PAULA: Does the polygraph automatically tell whether somebody is lying?

POLYGRAPH TECHNICIAN: It's a bit more complicated that than. The polygraph measures a person's physical response to a series of questions.

STEVE: Like if they sweat a lot or burp out their nose?

POLYGRAPH TECHNICIAN: More along the lines of recording their pulse rate, blood pressure, breathing and, yes, perspiration level. Many people's body functions change when they undergo the emotional stress of lying.

BURTON: I hope whoever stole my bike is undergoing some emotional stress!

MS. VERA: Thank you very much, Mr. Hanafin. You've been very informative. Class, walk single file to the exit.

(Ms. Vera turns and exits right with Burton, Paula, Janice, and Steve following behind and waving farewell to the Crime Lab Technicians who return the wave. At down right the children stop and huddle a moment.)

PAULA: I bet those red streaks are an important clue. Blood maybe!
JANICE: We'll need a lot more evidence than one tiny purple pen.
STEVE: I think there is a lot more going on here than just a stolen bike.
BURTON: *(looks at wristwatch)* You're right. It's almost time for lunch!
PAULA: *(looks left)* Hey! Isn't that your bike?

(DONNA enters from left, walking the bike and whistling nonchalantly.)

BURTON: Donna!
DONNA: Well, *there* you are, little brother! I've been looking all over for you!
BURTON: I've been looking all over for my bike!
DONNA: This old thing? *(thrusts bike at Burton)* I saw it lying on the ground in front of the drugstore — unlocked *and* unchained. If I hadn't come along in the nick of time and *rescued* it, somebody would have taken it for keeps. *(grabs pen from Steve's hand)* Hey! What are *you* doing with *my* purple pen?
STEVE: *Your* purple pen?
DONNA: *(displays fingernails)* It's got my candy-apple red nail polish on it, doesn't it? What's it doing in this icky plastic bag? Ewwww!

(Donna strides offstage right, holding bag at arm's length.)

JANICE: I guess that mystery is solved.
BURTON: Yeh, but not the *real* mystery.
PAULA: What's that?
BURTON: Of all the big sisters in the world, why did I end up with her?

(LIGHTS OUT.)

THE END

See You in Court!
(Legal Aid Lawyer)

Many lawyers specialize in a particular type of law, such as tax law, criminal law, environmental law, family law, constitutional law, and so forth. Legal aid lawyers work for the Legal Services Corporation, a part of the federal government that provides legal assistance to poor people in civil (not criminal) matters including family law, consumer fraud, housing, jobs, education, and entitlement benefits. After graduating from law school, many legal aid lawyers begin their careers as researchers or clerks for experienced lawyers. A legal aid lawyer may also frequently work with an organization such as the American Civil Liberties Union that takes cases involving constitutional law.

For information about a career as a legal aid lawyer, contact these sources:

http://www.ltsi.net/lsc/index.html (Legal Services Corporation)
http://www.abanet.org/hr/interns/home.html (Intern opportunities for legal aid and public service lawyers posted at the web site of the American Bar Association, 750 North Lake Shore Drive, Chicago, IL 60611. 312/988-5000.)

RUNNING TIME: 20 minutes

CAST: 15 actors, minimum 4 boys (•), 5 girls (+)

- + Paula
- • Burton
- + Janice
- • Steve
- + Judge Drake
-   Court Reporter
- + Roberta Hale (Burton's Cousin), a Legal Aid Lawyer
- • Martin Dreyfuss, Plaintiff
- + Carla Mansfield, Supervisor
- • Perry Dyer, Supervisor's Lawyer
-   4 Jury Members
-   Bailiff

STAGE SET: at down right is Roberta Hale's law office — two chairs and a desk with a lamp and several stacks of papers; at down left and center is a courtroom — judge's table, witness chair, four jury chairs behind rope barriers, a table for defendant and a table for plaintiff; four chairs for defendant, plaintiff and their lawyers; four chairs for spectators; a table and chair for court reporter

PROPS: several stacks of papers, lamp, two attaché cases, gavel, safety report, laptop computer

COSTUMES: Paula, Burton, Janice, and Steve wear standard grade-school attire (Spring season); Burton wears a baseball cap and Janice has a bookbag on her back; Roberta Hale wears a standard female attorney's court appearance outfit; Judge Drake wears black judge's robe; Perry Dyer wears a three-piece business suit; Carla Mansfield wears a business woman's work suit; Martin Dreyfuss wears a suit jacket, tie, dress shirt, and pants; Bailiff wears a bailiff uniform — khaki or brown shirt and pants with an I.D. nameplate on shirt front; Court Reporter wears a business suit; Jury Members wear casual and business clothes

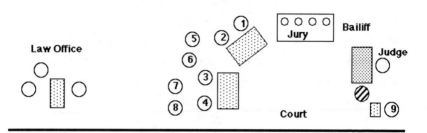

Stage Plan — *See You in Court!*

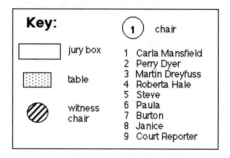

(LIGHTS UP RIGHT on the law office of ROBERTA HALE, LEGAL AID LAWYER, at down right. Roberta stands at her desk; JANICE and STEVE sit in chairs while PAULA and BURTON stand.)

BURTON: Hey, everybody, this is my cousin, Roberta Hale. She's a big-time lawyer! *(gestures around)* Just look at this swell office with all these books! They're the cases she's won in court!

ROBERTA HALE: Calm down, Burton. Actually, these books contain the laws of our state. A good lawyer has to be familiar with a lot of laws. And those books on the other shelf contain results of cases that have been tried in my law specialty.

PAULA: Can't a lawyer take any case?

ROBERTA HALE: Most lawyers try to become experts in one or two areas of the law. My specialty is employment law. Those are cases that involve disputes between employers and their workers, usually workers who have been fired or suffered mistreatment on the job.

JANICE: If somebody has been fired, how can they afford to hire a lawyer?

ROBERTA HALE: I am a legal aid lawyer, and I work for the Legal Services Corporation. We receive funding from the federal government to make sure people who don't have much money can still hire a good lawyer to represent their case in court.

STEVE: Are you going to try a case today?

ROBERTA HALE: Yes, I'm due in court at eleven o'clock. My client believes he was fired unjustly. He reported a defective product to his supervisor. Instead of fixing the product, the company fired my client.

BURTON: That sure isn't fair!

ROBERTA HALE: You and I might think so, but my job as a lawyer is to prove it to the court. Come on, we can't be late.

(LIGHTS OUT RIGHT, LIGHTS UP CENTER AND LEFT on courtroom where JUDGE DRAKE sits behind judge's table, A COURT REPORTER sits at a table next to witness chair typing into a laptop computer, A BAILIFF stands at up right, FOUR JURY MEMBERS sit in roped-off jury box, CARLA MANSFIELD and PERRY DYER sit at defendant's table and MARTIN DREYFUSS sits at plaintiff's table. Roberta Hale sits next to Martin

Dreyfuss; Steve, Paula, Janice, and Burton sit in chairs behind.)

BAILIFF: Adams County Superior Court Number One now in session. Case Number 55-96-00850, Martin Dreyfuss, Plaintiff, against Fun-O-Rama Toy Company. Honorable J.P. Drake, presiding.
JUDGE DRAKE: Are all parties present and with counsel?
ROBERTA HALE: Yes, your honor.
PERRY DYER: Yes, your honor.
JUDGE DRAKE: Good. The court will hear plaintiff's opening statement.

(Roberta Hale rises.)

ROBERTA HALE: My plaintiff's case is very simple, your honor. On July 30 of last year, Martin Dreyfuss, a product inspector at Fun-O-Rama Toy Company, discovered that the Wacky Jacky Hackysacky Doll had a serious safety flaw. Because of his efforts to have this flaw corrected, he was fired. Because of his efforts to protect the public from an unsafe toy, he was fired. Because of his efforts to make sure little children were not maimed and injured, he was fired. We ask the court for immediate redress. *(sits)*
JUDGE DRAKE: Mr. Dyer?

(Perry Dyer rises.)

PERRY DYER: The defendant asks the court to dismiss this case. Mr. Dreyfuss was fired because of poor job performance. His suit against the company is an ill-advised attempt to seek revenge. *(sits)*
JUDGE DRAKE: Plaintiff may call witnesses.

ROBERTA HALE: Carla Mansfield.

(Carla Mansfield rises, walks to witness chair, and sits; Roberta Hale walks to center of court and addresses her.)

ROBERTA HALE: Ms. Mansfield, what is your job title at the Fun-O-Rama Toy Company?
CARLA MANSFIELD: I am the Product Safety Supervisor, Doll Division.
ROBERTA HALE: When a product inspector informs you that a product has a safety flaw, what steps do you take?
CARLA MANSFIELD: I immediately inform the head of the engineering department, who assigns a team of engineers to examine the product and test it for safety.
ROBERTA HALE: What happens if the product is found to be unsafe?
CARLA MANSFIELD: The chief engineer informs me, and I inform the Vice President of Sales.
ROBERTA HALE: Who would then issue an order to stop selling the toy and have all defective toys recalled?
CARLA MANSFIELD: Yes. That is the standard procedure.
ROBERTA HALE: And what did the engineers find in this case?
CARLA MANSFIELD: I don't remember.
ROBERTA HALE: You don't remember?
CARLA MANSFIELD: I was on sick leave when they turned in their report.
ROBERTA HALE: You never saw the safety report?
CARLA MANSFIELD: I didn't say that — I, well, yes, I guess I saw the report.

(Roberta Hale walks to plaintiff's table and takes the safety report from her attache case, displaying it to the jury.)

ROBERTA HALE: And this report, a copy of which I hold in my hand, said the doll *did* have a flaw and should be recalled. Ms. Mansfield, did you then — according to standard procedure — inform the Vice President of Sales?

CARLA MANSFIELD: I, umm, I guess so.

ROBERTA HALE: Is that yes or no, Ms. Mansfield?

CARLA MANSFIELD: Ummm, actually no. I was going to, but then I went on vacation.

ROBERTA HALE: Will the court reporter please read back that last statement?

COURT REPORTER: "Ummm, actually no. I was going to, but then I went on vacation."

ROBERTA HALE: Thank you. That is all.

JUDGE DRAKE: Would the defense like to cross-examine the witness?

PERRY DYER: No, your honor.

JUDGE DRAKE: You may step down, Ms. Mansfield.

(Carla Mansfield returns to her seat at table.)

ROBERTA HALE: Plaintiff calls Martin Dreyfuss.

(Martin Dreyfuss walks to witness chair and sits; Roberta Hale walks to center of court and addresses him.)

ROBERTA HALE: Mr. Dreyfuss, what did your second inspection of the Wacky Jacky Hackysacky Doll reveal?

MARTIN DREYFUSS: The problem had not been corrected.

ROBERTA HALE: What did you do then?

MARTIN DREYFUSS: I went to my supervisor, Carla Mansfield, to tell her.

ROBERTA HALE: What did she say?

MARTIN DREYFUSS: She didn't say anything. She wouldn't see me.

ROBERTA HALE: She wouldn't see you?

MARTIN DREYFUSS: She refused to see me in person or accept my phone calls.

ROBERTA HALE: Did she give a reason for this?

MARTIN DREYFUSS: None.

ROBERTA HALE: So you decided to appeal to a higher level.

MARTIN DREYFUSS: I felt the problem was urgent. Children could be hurt. I couldn't have that on my conscience. So, I wrote a letter to the Vice President of Sales saying the toy should be recalled right away.

ROBERTA HALE: And two days later, you were fired.

MARTIN DREYFUSS: That is correct.

ROBERTA HALE: Thank you. That is all.

JUDGE DRAKE: Cross-examine, defense?

PERRY DYER: Yes, we would.

(Roberta Hale returns to her seat at table; Perry Dyer walks to center of court and addresses Martin Dreyfuss.)

PERRY DYER: Mr. Dreyfuss, is it not true that in the month before you were fired, you missed three days of work?

MARTIN DREYFUSS: It is true.

PERRY DYER: And the reason you missed work was...

MARTIN DREYFUSS: I went to St. Louis.

PERRY DYER: For what purpose?

MARTIN DREYFUSS: To attend a doll collector's convention. The biggest one in America!

PERRY DYER: And for this unexcused absence, Mr. Dreyfuss, you were given a warning from your supervisor?

MARTIN DREYFUSS: Yes. But I still found a safety flaw—

PERRY DYER: A warning that said you would be fired if you committed any other breaches of employee conduct?

MARTIN DREYFUSS: Well, yes. But—

PERRY DYER: But what, Mr. Dreyfuss? If you're quite finished interrupting, I'd like to continue.

MARTIN DREYFUSS: Well...sure.

PERRY DYER: I have no more questions. *(turns away and returns to his seat at table)*

JUDGE DRAKE: Do you wish to redirect, Ms. Hale?

ROBERTA HALE: *(rises)* No, your honor. I would like to give a summation to the jury.

JUDGE DRAKE: Proceed. You may step down, Mr. Dreyfuss.

(Martin Dreyfuss returns to his seat at table as Roberta Hale walks to center of court and addresses the jury.)

ROBERTA HALE: Ladies and gentlemen, Martin Dreyfuss was fired because he did his job and did it well. His job was to report unsafe toys to his supervisor. When his supervisor took no action to correct the situation, Martin Dreyfuss reported to *her* supervisor. And for this, he was fired.

(She pauses, faces the defendant's table.)

ROBERTA HALE: The defense would like you to consider Martin's brave and principled action a "breach of employee conduct." That in trying to force the Fun-O-Rama Toy Company to live up to its own safety standards, *he* was at fault.

(She walks to the plaintiff's table and points to Martin Dreyfuss.)

ROBERTA HALE: But in fact, Martin Dreyfuss cares a great deal about his job. He cares a great deal about the children — your children, my children — who play with the toys he must certify as safe. As a man of conscience and moral integrity, Martin Dreyfuss had no other choice but to go over his supervisor's head to preserve the public interest, and for this he was unjustly fired.

(She walks to the judge's table.)

ROBERTA HALE: Martin Dreyfuss is not alone in his beliefs. Many other court cases have established the right of employees to expose illegal or immoral activities of their employer — and to be protected from retribution. I call the court's attention to several cases decided by state supreme courts, among them McClanahan 1988, Phipps 1987, Palmer 1988, and Harless 1978.

(She turns to the jury.)

ROBERTA HALE: In conclusion, I ask the jury to find for my client, Martin Dreyfuss. Show him that you share his belief that a company must act responsibly toward its customers. And that the welfare of our children can never be put at risk. Thank you.

(She returns to her seat at table as Perry Dyer walks to center of court and addresses the jury.)

PERRY DYER: This is a simple case. According to company rules, Martin Dreyfuss violated procedure for reporting safety flaws. The plaintiff's attorney would have you believe that an employer has no right to discipline its employees. This is clearly a dangerous precedent. I ask you to dismiss this frivolous lawsuit against the Fun-O-Rama Toy Company.

(Perry Dyer returns to his seat at table, as the Jury Members rise and begin filing offstage up left.)

JUDGE DRAKE: Bailiff, escort the jurors to the jury room. Court is in recess. *(exits offstage down left)*

(Lawyers whisper with their respective clients; Court Reporter relaxes; Burton stands.)

BURTON: Wow, that was some trial! How do you think the jury is going to vote?

JANICE: I thought your cousin was very persuasive. And her facts were well-organized.

STEVE: Yeh, but did you see that other lawyer's suit? Wow, it sure looks expensive. I bet he wins a lot of cases.

PAULA: But a jury isn't supposed to be impressed by things like that! A jury is only supposed to consider the facts of the case!

STEVE: I guess so. But the main fact of *this* case is the other side's lawyer looks like the kind of lawyers on television that win their cases!

(Bailiff enters from up left followed by Jury Members, who return to their seats; Judge Drake enters from down left and sits in chair.)

JUDGE DRAKE: Has the jury reached a verdict?

JURY MEMBER #1: *(stands)* We have, your honor. We find the defendant, Fun-O-Rama Toy Company, guilty of illegally firing the plaintiff, Martin Dreyfuss.

BURTON & STEVE: Yahoo!

JUDGE DRAKE: *(slams gavel)* Order in the court! *(to Jury Member #1)* Have you set an award for judgment?

JURY MEMBER #1: Yes, your honor. Martin Dreyfuss is to be awarded two hundred thousand dollars in damages for lost wages and emotional distress. And he may have his job back, if he desires.

JUDGE DRAKE: Very good. Case closed. Defendant has thirty days to file a judgment appeal. *(exits offstage down left, followed by Court Reporter)*

(Bailiff escorts Jury Members offstage up left; Carla Mansfield and Perry Dyer exit offstage down left; Janice, Burton, Paula, and Steve gather around Martin Dreyfuss and Roberta Hale.)

STEVE: Congratulations, Mr. Dreyfuss.
MARTIN DREYFUSS: Thank you. I owe it all to my lawyer.
ROBERTA HALE: I didn't do anything special. I just researched the relevant information and presented it in a clear and logical manner.
PAULA: The other lawyer was kind of a bully. I don't think the jury liked that.
ROBERTA HALE: A jury is supposed to decide *only* on the testimony it hears. But in their hearts, they saw Martin Dreyfuss as a kind man who wanted to do everything he could to make safer toys.
JANICE: Well, I'm sure not going to buy that Wacky Jacy Hackysacky doll! It sounds like a menace!
BURTON: I wonder. My older sister has a birthday coming up. Mr. Dreyfuss, do you think the doll might perhaps come alive and strangle her?
ROBERTA HALE: Watch out, Burton! Or I'll be seeing *you* in court!

(All laugh. LIGHTS OUT.)

THE END

Yankee Doodle Had a Brick
(Brick Mason)

Brick masonry is one of the oldest careers in the world. The Pyramids of Egypt, the Great Wall of China, the Mayan temples of Mexico were all made by brick masons — as were the walls of your local fire station and many of your town's first sidewalks if it was settled in the late eighteenth or early nineteenth centuries. A modern brick mason works with many materials besides bricks (hollow concrete blocks, structural tiles, natural and artificial stone, and prefabricated masonry panels) to build walls, partitions, arches, fireplaces, chimneys, sidewalks, patios, and firebrick linings in industrial kilns and furnaces. Many brick masons learn the trade by working as helpers to experienced masons. Others enroll in apprenticeship programs that combine classroom instruction with up to four years of on-the-job training. Some masons take courses at community colleges and technical schools and earn a degree in construction management and technology.

For information about a career as a brick mason, contact these sources:

Brick Institute of America, 11490 Commerce Park Drive, Reston, VA 20191-1525. 703/620-0010.

http://www.omca.org/career.html (Ontario Masonry Training Centre)

http://leeca8.leeca.ohio.gov/LCJVS/masonry.html (Masonry Trades web site)

RUNNING TIME: 15 minutes

CAST: 10 actors, minimum 4 boys (•), 4 girls (+)

+	Paula	•	Mr. Hart (Janice's Father), Brick Mason
•	Burton	+	The Mayor
+	Janice	+	Yellow Thrush
•	Steve	•	Isaac Holcomb
			2 Bricklayers

STAGE SET: at down center is the sidewalk site — a four-foot by four-foot enclosure filled with sand and contained within a square of two-inch high wooden header boards; next to it stands a brickpile of twenty-thirty standard bricks; behind the site at mid center are two stools and a table to hold tools (level, rubber mallet, fanning trowel) and cardboard cutouts showing brick patterns

PROPS: seven hard hats, clipboard, level, rubber mallet, fanning trowel, hoe, four cardboard cutouts showing brick patterns, bucket of sand, broom, corn seed, seed pouch, snuff, snuff box, screed *

MUSIC: "I've Been Working on the Sidewalk, Yankee Doodle"

COSTUMES: Paula, Burton, Janice, and Steve wear standard grade-school attire (Spring season); Burton wears a baseball cap under his hard hat and Janice has a bookbag on her back; Mr. Hart and Two Bricklayers wear hard hats, jeans, T-shirts or work shirts, work boots; Mayor wears standard business woman's suit; Yellow Thrush is dressed as a eighteenth-century Native American of the Eastern Woodlands with a fringed buckskin dress, feathered headdress, beads, brown moccasins; Isaac Holcomb is dressed in mid-eighteenth-century artisan attire — blousy shirt, vest, knee breeches, buckle shoes (c.f., pictures of Benjamin Franklin, George Washington, etc.)

* A <u>screed</u> is a board used to level a sand surface; in its simplest form it is a two-inch by six-inch board a few inches longer in length than the area needing to be leveled. The bricklayer slides the screed back and forth along the header boards of the sidewalk surface to level the sand.

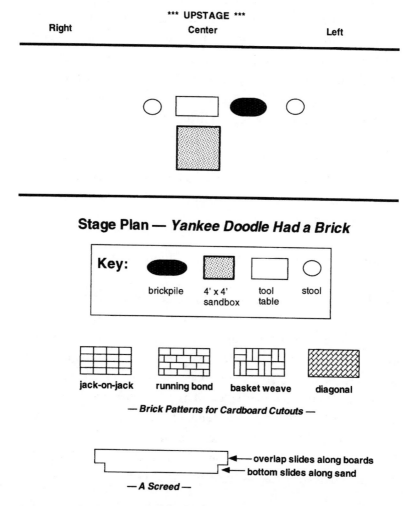

(LIGHTS UP FULL on JANICE, PAULA, BURTON, and STEVE standing at down right facing audience. They wear hard hats and sing "I've Been Working on the Sidewalk" while miming work motions with shovel and pickax.)

JANICE, PAULA, BURTON, & STEVE: *(sing)*
> I've been working on the sidewalk,
> All the livelong day!
> I've been working on the sidewalk,
> Just to pass the time away!
>
> Can't you hear the whistle calling,
> Calling so early in the morn?
> I've been working on the sidewalk,
> Mason, blow your horn!

PAULA: Hey, Janice, thanks for bringing us to watch your dad work today. What is he going to do here at the history museum?

JANICE: My dad is a brick mason, Paula. He is going to finish making a new sidewalk in the museum garden.

BURTON: That's cool! But why would anybody want to put a sidewalk in a garden?

PAULA: Obviously, Burton, so people don't park their cars on the flowers!

BURTON: Right! *(frowns)* Huh?

(MR. HART enters from right carrying a clipboard.)

MR. HART: Hi, kids!
BURTON, STEVE, & PAULA: Hi, Mr. Hart!
JANICE: Hi, Dad!

STEVE: *(twirls the hard hat on a finger)* These helmet thingies are neat!

MR. HART: That is called a "hard hat," Steve, and you'd better keep it on your head. It is an important piece of safety equipment for any construction job. Come on, let's see the site.

(Mr. Hart leads kids to the sidewalk site at down center; he lays the clipboard on the table and picks up a brick from the brickpile.)

MR. HART: Say, who knows where the first bricks were made?

BURTON: *(raises hand)* In Italy, for the brick pizza ovens?

STEVE: *(raises hand)* In Indianapolis for the Brickyard 400 auto race?

MR. HART: Sorry, guys, but bricks were first made a long time before that — about six thousand years ago in Mesopotamia in the Middle East. In America the first bricks were the adobe kind used by the Spanish in the Southwest. In the English colonies, brick making began in Virginia in 1611.

JANICE: My dad learned to be a brick mason from his dad.

MR. HART: And my dad learned from his dad, who learned from my great-grandfather. Our family has been building things with brick for a very long time.

PAULA: What exactly is a brick, Mr. Hart?

MR. HART: You dig clay from the ground, then crush and mix the clay with water. This mixture is molded into the basic brick shape, then burned in an oven called a kiln. The burning, then cooling off, makes the brick hard and strong.

(TWO BRICKLAYERS enter from left and cross to the

sidewalk site at down center; Bricklayer #1 carries a hoe, Bricklayer #2 carries a screed.)

MR. HART: Here comes my construction crew now.
BRICKLAYER #1: Morning, Mr. Hart.
BRICKLAYER #2: Fine day for working if it doesn't rain.
MR. HART: You bet!

(Bricklayer #1 stands at left of site and hoes the sand, smoothing it out; Bricklayer #2 kneels at right of site and begins using the screed to level the sand.)

MR. HART: Yesterday we prepared the base. We did the grading and edging and laid the sand bed that the bricks will go on. The next step is to do the screeding.
BRICKLAYER #2: *(holds up screed)* This is a screed — a board that pulls along the header boards and scrapes the sand until it is completely smooth and level.

(Bricklayer #1 lays down hoe and picks up a brick from brick pile.)

BRICKLAYER #1: This is a fine-looking brick, Mr. Hart.
BURTON: Aren't all bricks pretty much the same?
MR. HART: Not at all. There are about ten thousand different types of colors, textures, and shapes of brick. What we're using on this job are called "common bricks."
BRICKLAYER #1: And a special kind of common bricker is called a "clinker brick." *(displays brick)* See the black patches here and there along the surface? This is where the brick was over burned. It gives an old-time effect like cobblestone.
JANICE: And cobblestone is the kind of sidewalk and street paving that was popular when our town was founded.

MR. HART: That's right, Janice. The history museum wants this garden to be like just it was two hundred years ago.

(Bricklayer #2 lays aside the screed and addresses Mr. Hart.)

BRICKLAYER #2: How does that look, boss?

(Mr. Hart takes a level from the tool table and checks the sand surface.)

MR. HART: Good and true! Now let's lay some brick!
BRICKLAYER #1: Which laying pattern did the committee decide to use?
MR. HART: There were four finalists. Say, kids, hold up those cardboards!

(Janice, Paula, Steve, and Burton each pick up a cardboard cutout showing brick patterns and display them facing the audience.)

MR. HART: The names of the patterns are on the back. Read them off!
JANICE: My pattern is called "diagonal."
PAULA: I have the "running bond" pattern.
STEVE: My pattern is called "jack-on-jack."
BURTON: And mine is called "basket weave."
BRICKLAYER #2: My personal favorite!
MR. HART: In the end, the committee decided to use the running bond pattern. They felt it was more like the original sidewalk pattern.

(Kids set cardboards aside and Bricklayer #1 hands bricks to Bricklayer #2 who sets them on the sand in the

running bond pattern as Mr. Hart talks. After the bricks are laid, Bricklayer #1 takes the rubber mallet and taps them down level, while Bricklayer #2 scatters sand into joints and tamps it down with a fanning trowel.)

MR. HART: After the bricks have been laid, they are tapped into place with a rubber mallet. This is to make sure they are truly level. When bricks are all set, we fill in the joints — the spaces between the bricks — with fine sand. Then we scatter more sand over the bricks and let everything settle. In a few hours, we sweep the sand into joints, then sprinkle water over it all. After the sand dries, it will hold the bricks together better.

(Two Bricklayers finish and return tools to table.)

MR. HART: Good work, crew! Go ahead and rest a few minutes.

(Two Bricklayers sit on stools as MAYOR enters from left, followed by YELLOW THRUSH and ISAAC HOLCOMB.)

JANICE: Look, it's the Mayor!
MAYOR: Mr. Hart! How is the work going?
MR. HART: We're just about finished, Mayor. We'll be ready to re-open the museum right on schedule.
MAYOR: That is excellent. Look who I have with me today — two of our town founders.
YELLOW THRUSH: I am Yellow Thrush.
ISAAC HOLCOMB: And I am Isaac Holcomb. Glad to meet you all!
PAULA: Are you really both two hundred years old?
MAYOR: No, they are professional actors who present characters from history. They research how people in the

past dressed and ate and spoke and worked. Then they talk to visitors who come to the history museum and ask about our town's history.

YELLOW THRUSH: My tribe lived in this area for many hundreds of moons before there was a town.

ISAAC HOLCOMB: I am a tinsmith by trade down at Cobbler's Cross. Do you think King George is going to put another tax on colonial tea?

MAYOR: Yellow Thrush and Isaac Holcomb have come to bless the bricks.

YELLOW THRUSH: When any new thing is made, the spirits must receive thanks. I will offer corn seed because it represents the force of life.

(Yellow Thrush takes corn seed from pouch and scatters it across the sidewalk.)

ISAAC HOLCOMB: And I, being a jovial fellow, will ask the muse of song to spread her shield of safety over this vital public work. Strike up the band!

(Isaac Holcomb steps forward facing audience and sings. MUSIC: "Yankee Doodle." Steve, Paula, Burton, and Janice vocalize introductory march-rhythm drumbeats.)

JANICE, PAULA, BURTON, & STEVE: Brrrr-um-pum! Brrrr-um-pum! Brrrr-um-pum-pum!

ISAAC HOLCOMB: *(sings)*
    Yankee Doodle had a brick,
    He had a brick so rosy;
    When a redcoat came to town,
    He threw it at his nose-y!

ALL: *(sing)*
>Yankee Doodle had a brick,
>Yankee Doodle dandy;
>Yankee Doodle had a brick,
>He always kept it handy!

ISAAC HOLCOMB: *(sings)*
>Yankee Doodle went to war,
>A-riding on a pony;
>All that horse would ever eat
>Was bricks and macaroni!

ALL: *(sing)*
>Yankee Doodle had a brick,
>Yankee Doodle dandy;
>Yankee Doodle had a brick,
>He always kept it handy!

ISAAC HOLCOMB: *(sings)*
>When Yankee Doodle sailed to France,
>To swim he took a notion;
>He filled his hat with bricks galore
>And sank into the ocean!

(Isaac Holcomb leads Entire Cast marching offstage left.)

ALL: *(sing)*
>Yankee Doodle had a brick,
>Yankee Doodle dandy;
>Yankee Doodle had a brick,
>He always kept it handy!
>
>Yankee Doodle had a brick,
>Yankee Doodle dandy;

Yankee Doodle had a brick,
He always kept it handy!

(Last character has exited. LIGHTS OUT.)

THE END

Yankee Doodle Had a Brick
(music: traditional, words: L.E. McCullough)

Lights, Camera, Traction!
(Television Director)

When you watch your favorite television show, you probably notice only the actors. But making even a simple television program requires the hard work of dozens of people you'll never see. A television director is in charge of making the show happen from the opening scene to the final credit and needs to know a little bit about every aspect of the production from costuming to lighting to acting and camera angles. Most directors work from a script prepared by a writer or team of writers. Then it's the director's job to assemble the actors and the technical crew to support them. Most people who work in television get their first jobs as interns or production assistants whose job is to do almost anything needed to be done — often at a moment's notice — to help the director keep the show on schedule. It may seem like a thankless job, but it is a good way to understand all aspects of television production. Many directors start out filming commercials or directing the news at a local television station. Other directors begin by directing plays in small theatres or simply by making their own films and videos that eventually win them a chance to direct for a television network or film studio. Though some colleges have courses in directing and television and film work, a good way to start is to make films and videos of your own with your friends and family.

For information about a career as a director, contact these sources which have information about directing classes and opportunities:

National Association of Broadcasters, 1771 N Street NW, Washington DC 20036. 202/429-5300.

http://www.afionline.org/cover/contents.html (American Film Institute)

http://www.filmarts.org/ (Film Arts Foundation)

http://www.dga.org/ (Directors Guild of America)

http://www.arts-online.com/sdnc.htm (Stage Directors and Choreographers, 1501 Broadway, #1701, New York, NY 10036. 212/302-5359.)

RUNNING TIME: 20 minutes

CAST: 18 actors, minimum 3 boys (•), 4 girls (+)

+	Paula	+	Sara Whittaker, Television Director
•	Burton	+	Anna, Production Assistant
+	Janice		Grip
•	Steve		Camera Operator
•	Mr. Brooks, Teacher		Audio Engineer
	Editor		Prop Master
	Gaffer		Makeup Artist
	Hairstylist		Willy Bear, TV Show Host
	Costume Designer		Announcer (offstage)
			Vocal Chorus (offstage)

STAGE SET: At center is a long grey backdrop that frames the Studio Set — 4-foot by 4-foot stage 6-10 inches high on which stands a stool and a small table; a standing ladder is at the right corner of the stage, a studio camera (or facsimile) is positioned a few feet to the left and a camrail track is drawn on the floor in front of the stage; midway through the play a sign reading "The Willy Bear Show" with a goofy bear head graphic will be hung over the backdrop or attached to its top. At left is the Backstage Set — a mobile clothes rack and a table with a makeup palette and a wig rest. At right is the Control Room Set — a stool and a table with a mixing board (or facsimile) and a headset.

PROPS: clipboard, pen, socket wrench, screwdriver, microphone and cable, three pairs of headsets, comb, wig rest, makeup brushes, makeup palette, plastic fish bowl, cardboard sign reading "APPLAUSE!", glass of grape juice

EFFECT: Sound — prerecorded audience applause

MUSIC: "The Willy Bear Theme Song"

COSTUMES: Paula, Burton, Janice, and Steve wear standard grade-school attire (Spring season); Burton wears a baseball cap and Janice has a bookbag on her back; Mr. Brooks wears a standard male teacher's school outfit; Camera Operator, Audio Engineer, and Sara Whittaker have headsets; Sara Whittaker wears a standard business woman's outfit; Anna, Grip, Camera Operator, Audio Engineer, Editor, Prop Master, Gaffer, Costume Designer, Makeup Artist, and Hairstylist wear casual attire, with Makeup Artist and Hairstylist wearing cosmetician smocks and Grip and Gaffer perhaps having a tool belt around their waists; Willy Bear is dressed in a bear costume with a detachable head featuring a big silly grin

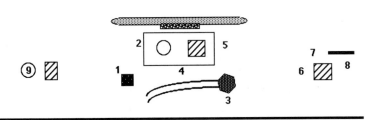

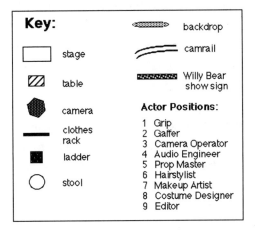

Stage Plan — *Lights, Camera, Traction!*

Key:
- stage
- table
- camera
- clothes rack
- ladder
- stool
- backdrop
- camrail
- Willy Bear show sign

Actor Positions:
1. Grip
2. Gaffer
3. Camera Operator
4. Audio Engineer
5. Prop Master
6. Hairstylist
7. Makeup Artist
8. Costume Designer
9. Editor

(LIGHTS UP RIGHT on JANICE, PAULA, BURTON, STEVE, and MR. BROOKS standing at down right.)

MR. BROOKS: Has anyone been on television before?

BURTON: *(raises hand)* I was on the news once. My brother won a go-kart race and ran over my foot on the last lap. They showed me getting first-aid.

MR. BROOKS: That's nice, Burton. Today we are going to

visit a real television studio and see an actual show broadcast live. *(looks offstage right)* Here comes our guide!

(ANNA enters from right.)

ANNA: Hi, everybody! My name is Anna. I'm a Production Assistant here at W-O-O-F television.
MR. BROOKS: What does a Production Assistant do, Anna?
ANNA: A little bit of everything. Follow me, and we'll go to the studio.

(LIGHTS OUT RIGHT, LIGHTS UP CENTER on Studio Set where SARA WHITTAKER, TELEVISION DIRECTOR, stands talking with the CAMERA OPERATOR. Sara Whittaker holds a clipboard and writes on it as Anna brings the Class to down center.)

ANNA: Ms. Whittaker, our visitors are here.
SARA WHITTAKER: Hi! I'm Sara Whittaker. I'm a Director here at the station. My job is to make sure what happens in this studio gets inside your television set. Let's take a tour. First, meet our Camera Operator.
CAMERA OPERATOR: Howdy! I'm just checking my lenses to make sure they're clean. Anna, can you get me a green filter from the supply room?
ANNA: Sure. *(exits left)*

(Sara Whittaker leads the group along the camrail to the ladder on which the GRIP is standing, using a socket wrench to fixing a light above.)

SARA WHITTAKER: If we follow this camrail — that's a track the camera is attached to so it can glide smoothly from one side of the studio to the other — we come to our Grip.

GRIP: *(waves from ladder)* Hello, down there! How's the weather?

SARA WHITTAKER: A grip is the person who sets up the lights and mobile cameras.

GRIP: A grip is part electrician, part chimpanzee, and totally nuts!

(Sara Whittaker points to the GAFFER who is kneeling on the floor working with a screwdriver under the corner of the stage.)

SARA WHITTAKER: Over here by the stage is our Gaffer.

GAFFER: I'm the head electrician on the set. Right now I'm installing a new outlet under the stage.

(Sara Whittaker points to the AUDIO ENGINEER who is in front of the stage adjusting a microphone in his hand.)

SARA WHITTAKER: Making sure we can hear what the actors say is our Audio Engineer.

AUDIO ENGINEER: Right now I'm getting this new microphone ready to go for today's show. *(speaks into microphone)* Testing one-two-three, testing!

(Sara Whittaker points to the PROP MASTER who is at the upper end of the stage moving the table a tiny bit here and there.)

SARA WHITTAKER: In charge of all the furniture and objects on the set is the Prop Master. Gee, Sam, you've been working with that table for the last ten minutes!

PROP MASTER: Well, you know, Sara, Mr. Willy Bear is awfully precise about where his supper table sits.

PAULA: Willy Bear!

BURTON: This must be the set for *The Willy Bear Show!*

SARA WHITTAKER: Do you guys like *The Willy Bear Show?*

STEVE: Like it? We watch it every single day! I can't believe this is the Willy Bear set!

JANICE: *(raises hand)* I think *The Willy Bear Show* is a bit juvenile.

SARA WHITTAKER: Well, of course it is. It's for kids! And you kids are in luck, because today we're going to do a taping of the show with Mr. Willy Bear in person!

PAULA, BURTON, & STEVE: Yayyyy!

SARA WHITTAKER: First, we'd better check backstage. Follow me.

(LIGHTS OUT CENTER, LIGHTS UP LEFT as Sara Whittaker leads the Class to the Backstage Set at mid left where the HAIRSTYLIST, MAKEUP ARTIST, and COSTUME DESIGNER are gathered around a table — the Hairstylist is combing the hair on a wig, the Makeup Artist is dabbing makeup brushes into a makeup palette, the Costume Designer is adjusting clothes on a clothes rack.)

PAULA: Is this Willy Bear's dressing room?

SARA WHITTAKER: It sure is. And this is the show's Hairstylist.

HAIRSTYLIST: Hi! I make sure the actors have the right kind of hairstyle that fits their character.

MAKEUP ARTIST: I'm the Makeup Artist. I have to put everyone's face on *and* make sure they have the right skin texture for the camera and lighting.

COSTUME DESIGNER: And I'm the Costume Designer. My

job is to select the clothes and accessories we need for each show.

SARA WHITTAKER: *(checks her watch)* Speaking of which, we've got just four minutes till showtime. I'd better get to the control room and make sure we're ready to roll.

(Anna enters from left, breathless, and runs up to Sara Whittaker.)

ANNA: Ms. Whittaker, Ms. Whittaker!

SARA WHITTAKER: What is it, Anna?

ANNA: There's been an accident on the set! One of the guests bumped into the ladder the grip was using!

SARA WHITTAKER: Was anyone hurt?

ANNA: No, but the set is a mess!

SARA WHITTAKER: Well, let's get it cleaned up. Come on!

(LIGHTS OUT LEFT, LIGHTS UP CENTER as Anna, Sara Whittaker, and the Class go to the Studio Set at center; the ladder is down, the table is knocked over and an empty fish bowl lies on the floor. The Gaffer is helping the Grip get up from the floor, and the Prop Master is searching for something on the ground.)

SARA WHITTAKER: What happened?

GAFFER: It was the pig! That pig is insane!

SARA WHITTAKER: The guest pig from Porter's Pig Park?

GRIP: That darn pig tore through here like a porkpie tornado! Knocked me off the ladder—

GAFFER: And knocked over Mr. Willy Bear's supper table!

ANNA: The fish bowl is empty!

BURTON: Uncle Goldie!

PROP MASTER: I'm looking for him! He can't have gotten too far.

LIGHTS, CAMERA, TRACTION!

SARA WHITTAKER: Find that fish! And tell the pig he's off the show!
BURTON: Uncle Goldie is my favorite character! You've got to find him!
MR. BROOKS: They're doing everything they can, Burton. Just calm down.
JANICE: I always thought Uncle Goldie was too clever for this show. I think he's using the confusion as a chance to escape.
ANNA: What do we tell the audience if we can't find Uncle Goldie, Ms. Whittaker?
SARA WHITTAKER: Make up a story. He's...he's...
STEVE: He's gone fishing!
SARA WHITTAKER: He's taking the day off. Anna, go to the pet store and get another goldfish. All right, crew, let's get ready! We're on in three minutes!

(LIGHTS OUT CENTER, LIGHTS UP RIGHT as Sara Whittaker and the Class go to the Control Room where the EDITOR sits on a stool, cueing up levels on a mixing board; a headset lies on the table. Sara Whittaker stands above the Editor, and the Class stands behind them to the right.)

SARA WHITTAKER: This is the control room, and this is our Editor.
EDITOR: *(without looking up from board)* Glad to meet you.
SARA WHITTAKER: We're in a bit of a crunch today. How's it going?
EDITOR: I'm not getting any sound from the main microphone.
SARA WHITTAKER: No sound!?! What? Why?
EDITOR: No sound.
SARA WHITTAKER: Who? When? Where?

(Audio Engineer dashes to the table from behind the center backdrop.)

AUDIO ENGINEER: The pig chewed through the main microphone cable!
SARA WHITTAKER: Lay down another cable!
AUDIO ENGINEER: I already sent Anna to get one!
SARA WHITTAKER: Good thinking! *(looks at watch)* Where did you send her — Argentina?
AUDIO ENGINEER: I'll check the other inputs. *(dashes back behind center backdrop)*
STEVE: Maybe Willy Bear knows sign language.
SARA WHITTAKER: Less than two minutes, people.
BURTON: I'm getting very nervous!

(Sara Whittaker picks up the headset and shouts into it.)

SARA WHITTAKER: Backstage! Is Willy Bear ready?
COSTUME DESIGNER: *(offstage)* His head is missing!
SARA WHITTAKER: What!?!
COSTUME DESIGNER: *(offstage)* I can't find his head! It was here five minutes ago!
PAULA: That darn pig! If he's eaten Mr. Willy Bear's head—
SARA WHITTAKER: Somebody bring me the head of Willy Bear!
COSTUME DESIGNER: *(offstage)* Oh, Anna just brought a replacement from storage. It's going to be tight, but I think it'll fit. Mmmph!
SARA WHITTAKER: One minute, people, less than one minute! Do we have sound?
EDITOR: We have sound! Thanks, Anna!
SARA WHITTAKER: Is the set ready?
PROP MASTER: *(offstage)* Set is ready!
EDITOR: Twenty seconds, Ms. Whittaker.

SARA WHITTAKER: Camera one, are you ready?

CAMERA OPERATOR: *(offstage, garbled)* Rwggggbrrrkkkkzzzz...

SARA WHITTAKER: Camera one, we can't hear you! Are you ready?

CAMERA OPERATOR: *(offstage)* Ready on one!

EDITOR: Ten seconds.

SARA WHITTAKER: Places, everyone! Cue theme music.

MAKEUP ARTIST: *(offstage)* Mr. Willy Bear, come back! Your nose is on crooked!

EDITOR: Five seconds.

SARA WHITTAKER: Anna, cue audience applause!

EDITOR: Three, two, one—

SARA WHITTAKER: Showtime!

ANNOUNCER: *(offstage)* And now, cubs and cubettes, it's time for *The Willy Bear Show*!

(LIGHTS UP CENTER; *the plastic fishbowl is on the table, and a sign reading "The Willy Bear Show" with a goofy bear head graphic has been hung over the backdrop or attached to its top; from behind the backdrop bounds* WILLY BEAR *in full costume, lumbering onto the stage and flailing his front paws in the air as Anna stands at down center holding a sign toward audience that reads "APPLAUSE!"* SOUND: *prerecorded audience applause.* MUSIC: *"The Willy Bear Theme Song." Applause and music fade, Anna drops sign and runs behind backdrop as Camera Operator keeps camera on Willy Bear, who freezes in place.*)

VOCAL CHORUS: *(offstage, sing)*
He's big and brown and furry,
But he never has to worry,
Cause he is Mister Willy Bear!

SARA WHITTAKER: *(takes off headset)* Whew! That was a close one!
JANICE: Is it this hectic every day, Ms. Whittaker?
SARA WHITTAKER: Oh, today was a *good* day!

(Anna walks up to Control Room with a tall glass of grape juice and gives it to Sara Whittaker.)

ANNA: Here's your daily five o'clock grape juice, Ms. Whittaker.
SARA WHITTAKER: Thank you, Anna. You're a lifesaver.
PAULA: Gosh, a television director's job is a lot of hard work. You have to keep track of every single detail.
MR. BROOKS: And the show couldn't succeed without everyone working as a team.
SARA WHITTAKER: He's right, kids. On the Willy Bear team, the most important member isn't the star or the person with the biggest title. It's—
JANICE: Anna, the Production Assistant!
SARA WHITTAKER: Anna, take a bow!

(LIGHTS UP FULL as Anna steps to down center and bows as Entire Cast comes onstage and applauds. SOUND: prerecorded audience applause. LIGHTS OUT.)

THE END

Reach for the Stars
(Epilogue)

If you are doing two or more of these plays — perhaps even replicating the field trip sequence of the characters themselves — *Reach for the Stars* is a nice way to wrap things up. It is a short playlet that can be performed after any of the plays, offering a chance for your actors to reflect on what they've learned from seeing people at work.

RUNNING TIME: 10 minutes

CAST: 6 actors, minimum 3 boys (•), 3 girls (+)
- + Paula
- • Burton
- + Janice
- • Steve
- + Ms. Vera, Teacher
- • Mr. Brooks, Teacher

STAGE SET: at down center a semicircle of chairs flanked at each end by a high stool

MUSIC: "Reach for the Stars" (can be sung *a cappella* or with accompaniment)

COSTUMES: Paula, Burton, Janice, and Steve wear standard grade-school attire (Spring season); Burton wears a baseball cap and Janice has a bookbag at her side; Ms. Vera wears a standard female teacher's school outfit; Mr. Brooks wears a standard male teacher's school outfit

| Right | *** UPSTAGE *** Center | Left |

Stage Plan — *Reach for the Stars*

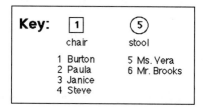

(LIGHTS UP FULL on JANICE, PAULA, BURTON, and STEVE sitting in a semicircle of chairs at down center facing the audience. MR. BROOKS and MS. VERA each sit on a stool on either side facing the students.)

MS. VERA: We've certainly been on some exciting field trips this semester, haven't we? We got to see people at work — people actually doing their jobs and then explaining what they did and why. What are some of the things you liked best about seeing people at work?

JANICE: *(raises hand)* I liked seeing people imagine and make new things, like the robotics engineers.

PAULA: *(raises hand)* I liked seeing people make beautiful things, like Janice's dad and his brick masons.

STEVE: *(raises hand)* I liked the people who put puzzles together, like the crime lab technicians and Paula's mom doing her newspaper reporting.

BURTON: *(raises hand)* I liked seeing people at work have fun, like my Uncle Leo, the pastry chef. Oh, and I liked the animal rescue agents a lot, too. They had fun every time they helped an animal.

MR. BROOKS: What did you learn about working? What did you learn about the kind of skills you might need to be a good worker?

(A slight pause as students ponder, then Steve raises his hand.)

STEVE: Burton's cousin, the legal aid lawyer, showed that knowing how to do research is important.

BURTON: I learned that an emergency medical technician has to be alert and calm.

STEVE: And so do piano tuners and television directors!

(Everyone chuckles.)

PAULA: Crime lab work and piano tuning both have a lot of detail to pay attention to.

BURTON: To be a newspaper reporter you have to be detailed and determined and find out all the facts.

JANICE: Teamwork is really important, especially on a tugboat.

PAULA: And at a television station.

STEVE: Right! Everybody has to pitch in and do their share, or the ship —

BURTON: Or show —

STEVE: Will sink.

PAULA: The park ranger and animal rescue agents showed that it's important to respect nature.

JANICE: Standing up for what you know is right is important. And helping other people stand up for their rights, like a legal aid lawyer does for her clients.

STEVE: All the people we met really loved their work. Even if the work was hard, they seemed happy doing it.

BURTON: Maybe as kids they had something they cared about a lot. And when they grew up, they made it their work.

MS. VERA: Who knows what they want to do when they grow up?

(No response as students ponder.)

MR. BROOKS: Does anybody know what they *don't* want to do?

STEVE: *(loud whisper)* Be a teacher?

(Everyone laughs heartily.)

PAULA: We made up a song about going on our field trips. Can we sing it?

MS. VERA: Certainly.

(PAULA and JANICE stand and start singing; STEVE and BURTON stand and join in at third line. MUSIC: "Reach for the Stars.")

PAULA & JANICE: *(sing)*
　Reach for the stars, they're yours for the taking;
　Reach for the stars, someday wonders you'll be making;

PAULA, JANICE, STEVE, & BURTON: *(sing)*
> Reach for the stars, let them guide you to greatness;
> Reach for the stars, and they'll always shine brightly for you.

(Entire Cast stands, faces audiences, and sings.)

ENTIRE CAST: *(sing)*
> Follow your dream, wherever it leads you;
> Follow your dream, let it nourish and feed you;
> Follow your dream, never turn from its calling;
> Follow your dream, and you'll find your true way in the world.

PAULA, JANICE, & MS. VERA: *(sing)*
> Reach for the stars!

STEVE, BURTON, & MR. BROOKS: *(sing)*
> Follow your dream!

PAULA, JANICE, & MS. VERA: *(sing)*
> Reach for the stars!

STEVE, BURTON, & MR. BROOKS: *(sing)*
> Follow your dream!

ENTIRE CAST: *(sing)*
> Reach for the stars and follow the light of your dream!

PAULA & JANICE: *(sing)*
> Your dream…your dream…

(LIGHTS OUT.)

THE END

Reach for the Stars
(words & music by L.E. McCullough)

Reach for the Stars, pg. 2

© L.E. McCullough 1998

The Author

L.E. McCULLOUGH, PH.D. has worked as a journalist, radio announcer, concert promoter, ad copy writer, teacher, librarian, landscaper, busboy, coupon cutter, book publisher, musician, and cat rancher. A playwright, composer, and ethnomusicologist whose studies in music and folklore have spanned cultures throughout the world, Dr. McCullough is the Administrative Director of the Humanities Theatre Group at Indiana University-Purdue University at Indianapolis. Winner of the 1995 Playwrights' Preview Productions Emerging Playwright Award for his stage play *Blues for Miss Buttercup*, he is the author of *The Complete Irish Tinwhistle Tutor*, *Favorite Irish Session Tunes*, and *St. Patrick Was a Cajun*, three highly acclaimed music instruction books, and has performed on the soundtracks for the PBS specials *The West* and *Lewis and Clark*. Since 1991 Dr. McCullough has received forty awards in thirty-one national literary competitions and had 178 poem and short story publications in ninety North American literary journals. He is a member of The Dramatists Guild, American Conference for Irish Studies, Southeastern Theatre Conference, and National Middle School Association. His books for Smith and Kraus include: *Plays of the Songs of Christmas*, *Stories of the Songs of Christmas*, *Ice Babies in Oz* (character monologues), *Plays of America from American Folklore, Vol. 1 & 2*, *Plays of the Wild West, Vol. 1 & 2*, *Plays from Fairy Tales*, *Plays from Mythology*, *Plays of Exploration and Discovery*, and *Anyone Can Produce Plays with Kids*.